PLAY GREAT GOLF

PLAY
GREAT
GOLF

Mastering the Fundamentals
of Your Game

ARNOLD PALMER

BRISTOL
PARK
BOOKS

First Bristol Park Books edition published in 1998.

Bristol Park Books
A division of BBS Publishing Corporation
386 Park Avenue South
New York, NY 10016

Bristol Park Books is a registered trademark of BBS Publishing Corporation.

Published by arrangement with Arnold Palmer Enterprises, Inc.

Designed by Stanley S. Drake/Folio Graphics Co., Inc.

Library of Congress Catalog Card Number: 97-77672

ISBN: 0-88486-191-0

Printed in the United States of America

To the frustrated golfers all over the world

CONTENTS

Acknowledgments

Any book worth its salt comes together through the talents of many people. I thank them all for getting *Play Great Golf* into the bookstores, but single out for special praise Ken Van Kampen of *Golf Magazine* and old friend Desmond Tolhurst for their important editorial assistance; Leonard Kamsler, the veteran golf photographer, for the new instructional pictures; Dom Lupo, the veteran golf illustrator, for the fine illustrations; and Angela Miller and David Gibbons of IMG Publishing, who oversaw the project. I also relied on the counsel and supervision of three long-time business associates—Alastair Johnston, Bev Norwood and Doc Giffin.

I thank Jim Fitzgerald, the editor at Dolphin Books, and Jeffrey Peisch, the executive producer at Vestron Video. My appreciation, too, goes to Terry Jastrow, his assistants and technicians, along with Bob Bagley, Jane Little and the staff of Trans World International, who, in concert, created and produced the two-hour video package that goes hand in hand with this book.

—ARNOLD PALMER

Introduction

I've written this book with one objective in mind: to help you play great golf. In the course of this book, I'll show you the Five Fundamentals of the golf swing and how to attain them. I'll teach you how to trim your score by mastering the shots needed around the green as well as how to prepare mentally to hit your best shots. Planning a playing strategy that suits *your* playing skills also will be covered, along with ways to get the most from your practice sessions.

If you read carefully and put my methods to work, you'll be able to trim as many as fifteen strokes from your handicap, even if you only have limited athletic ability.

Too good to be true, you say? I don't think so. Any golfer can score in the eighties, and a good many in the seventies, *if* they're willing to take the time to learn the fundamentals of golf.

"Sure," you're thinking, "this is probably another in-depth impossible-to-comprehend analysis of every part of the swing from A to Z. I might as well stop right here. No way I'll ever understand or be able to apply any of this."

Well, you're wrong. Don't stop; instead, read on.

I'm not saying that golf is a simple game—anyone who has tried it certainly knows it isn't. I am saying that by mastering and using a few of my simple techniques, the game itself is a lot easier.

The fundamentals of golf are, in fact, quite simple, contrary to the many complex theories that abound. As simple as the fundamentals are, they still take hard work to master. You have to put in some time on the practice ground; but if you do, you'll find, as I have, that it's well worth the effort.

I'm aware that my viewpoint is a minority one, especially in this day and age where even computers have been put to work to analyze and critique the golf swing. Ask any of your golfing buddies to explain his or her theory of the swing to you or pick up and read any other golf instruction book. The chances are, first, you'll get confused; second, you'll get discouraged. You'll run into intricate analyses on nearly every movement of the body, from the start of the takeaway to the finish of the follow-through. Often, these theories conflict or are so complicated that they leave the player at a loss over what to believe.

The accepted view is that the game of golf is complex, difficult, and inherently frustrating.

I just don't buy that. Playing great golf to me is like taking an automobile trip. First, you learn to drive the car. Once that's accomplished, you determine the easiest route to your destination. And just as most of us successfully have learned to drive a car, I believe that most of us can just as easily learn to drive a golf ball. Couple consistently good ball-striking with a sound method of negotiating the golf course, and you'll be playing great golf.

It doesn't sound too difficult—and it isn't.

This book presents a fresh, new look at the game of golf, a view so uncomplicated and basic that it undoubtedly will seem novel to a lot of golfers, especially those who have read and rejected other instruction books. If you make the effort to consider my approach carefully, I firmly believe it will help you form an entirely new attitude towards your golf game. If you combine this approach with good, old-fashioned hard work, you could lower your score further than you've ever dreamed.

My views on the game aren't ones that have been molded slowly through years of playing and practicing. They are based on the simple fundamentals taught to me by my father, Deacon Palmer, who was head pro and greenkeeper at the Latrobe Country Club in western Pennsylvania, where I grew up.

Pap believed in keeping the game as simple as possible. He felt that if a player mastered certain fundamentals, then his swing and his entire game would develop naturally.

The one thing my father always stressed, though, was practice. To him, the *brain* could learn the basics of golf from reading or watching, but practice taught the *body* what they were. He'd be the first to point out that nothing, not even a book by his son, could take the place of getting out and hitting golf balls. It's how I learned, and how you should as well.

So read on. If you possess the burning desire to play great golf, along with a willingness to work hard at your game, you'll discover the secrets that I learned from Pap long ago, that playing great golf is not as difficult as it might appear, and that the game is a lifelong joy to play when you find out how easy it actually can be.

A photo of my father, Deacon Palmer, and me at the Latrobe Country Club in the early sixties.

PART I

THE

FIVE

FUNDAMENTALS

Countless words have been written or spoken about the golf swing: how to hit the ball farther; how to hit it straighter; how to find out what's wrong with your swing and how to correct it when you do; and how to construct a picture-perfect swing. Despite the many theories, there still is little agreement on the subject of the so-called correct swing, much less on how to teach or learn it.

Golfers buy books, take lessons, watch video tapes, and attend schools with little improvement in their games to show for their efforts. Most remain dissatisfied with their ball-striking and scoring and never reach their actual scoring potential.

My pro-amateur tournament partners are generally extremely confused and frustrated by the notion of, or the actual act of, the swing. A lot of that is due to the conflicting ideas they'd been exposed to. I see golfers freeze at address for minutes on end as dozens of different swing keys race through their minds. The shot they ultimately hit is rarely worth the wait.

WHAT'S THE SECRET?

Ask ten recreational golfers what the secret of the swing is and you probably will get ten different answers, all wrong and many contradictory.

Here are a sample of the questions that have been posed to me by pro-am partners. They illustrate the general uncertainty among club golfers today about how to swing:

What is the shape of the correct swing, upright or flat?

How much turn, or body rotation, should the correct swing have?

How do I transfer my weight into the ball?

When do I release my wrists on the downswing, and how much?

Does the correct swing draw or fade the ball?

There probably are almost as many questions as there are golfers. But in this book, I want to show you that these kinds of questions not only are irrelevant to developing a good swing, they actually are detrimental.

Worrying about individual segments of a swing usually does little more than obstruct the motion of a good, solid swing. The proper golf swing, from start to finish, takes less than one-and-a-half seconds. There's no time to think of dozens of swing keys.

THE SWING IS A WHOLE

The swing should be looked at as a *whole*. The key to developing this whole-swing motion depends on the mastery of a few, simple fundamentals. Once you understand and employ them, the swing happens naturally and automatically, with no conscious effort or thought on your part.

There is no such thing as one correct swing that every golfer should try to imitate. In fact, the "perfect swing" myth keeps many golfers from playing great golf.

Instead, every swing should be as individual as the player himself. You may know two friends who both hit the ball well with two radically different-looking swings. That's why, although good swings share certain basics, in many ways they can vary tremendously.

If you still don't believe me, look at the swings of some of the top golfers on the Professional Golfers Association Tour over the years. Compare Jack Nicklaus to Lee Trevino to Johnny Miller. You'll see that very different-looking swings can be equally effective in achieving excellent golf shots. Despite having different body shapes, varying body turns, more or less wrist action, and different types of ball flight, these three pros produce the shots it takes to play great golf. Explain that, if you will, if you're an advocate of the "perfect swing" theory.

The reason these different-looking swings have produced such outstanding results lies in the fundamentals that are the basis for all good golf swings—the same fundamentals that my father taught me. Ironically, they often are overlooked in the quest for the perfect swing. Although most golfers believe that a uniform technique is necessary, they often ignore the very elements that actually are uniform among good swings.

JUST FIVE FUNDAMENTALS

These are the Five Fundamentals inherent in all good golf swings. You should try to incorporate them into your swing:

The Grip: the way you hold the club. There is one correct grip, and good golf is impossible without it

The Address: the relationship between the position of your feet, your balance, the club, and the ball at address

The Takeaway: the path of the club and arms during the start of the swing

The Still Head: the position of the head during the swing

Acceleration: the increasing speed at which the clubhead moves through the ball

It is impossible to put too much emphasis on the value of these five elements. If you work to master each of them, the rest of your swing will take care of itself. Your individual swing will automatically develop, based on your physical ability, age, body type, and style of play.

The results will come shining forth in your game. You'll enjoy hitting the ball more because you'll be hitting it where you want it to go with maximum power. Forget about all of the technical questions and theories that the analytic players use.

It's my firm belief that if every serious golfer took the time and made the effort to learn fully these five swing fundamentals, there wouldn't be anyone shooting above 90.

Still in doubt? I challenge you to invest the time and effort to see if I'm right. A day will come when you'll look back and be glad you did. I know I am right.

Before I begin to explain how to get started on the Five Fundamentals, I would like to add one last word toward debunking the "perfect swing" myth. Since I began playing golf on the PGA Tour, golf writers and commentators alike have expressed their opinions that my swing is "unorthodox," "weird," or just plain wrong. They go on to say that as a result of this, average players can't learn from my game and that I'm a bad influence on those who play recreational golf.

I disagree. It is not my premise to try to show you how to copy my swing move for move—that's completely opposite to my teaching convictions. What I want to do is give you the proper building blocks to construct your own swing and nothing more.

So read on and begin the process. The sooner you start, the sooner you'll be finished.

When you're finished, your swing probably will not look exactly like mine, but I promise you it will be just as functional.

1
The Grip

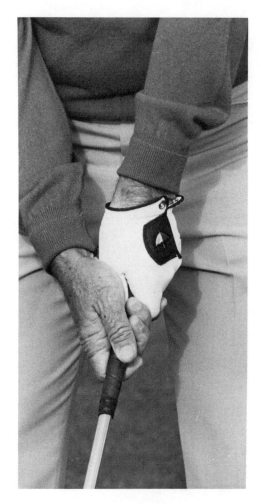

L et's start off by getting a club into your hands—the right way. The first of the Five Fundamentals is the grip, and it's crucial to have a good one to have much success at golf.

My father taught me the correct way to grip the club when I was three years old, and I've used it ever since. A good grip allows your hands to work together, creates the correct wrist action, and ensures square contact with the ball. It also gives you control of your club while leaving your muscles free and easy, ready to make a good swing. The bottom line is, without a good grip, your chances of putting the clubhead flush on the ball are extremely limited, no matter how good your swing is.

In contrast, a poor grip leads to your hands fighting each other during your swing. Excessive wrist action results in wayward shots: You either lose control of the club or have to grip so tightly you lose clubhead speed and power.

A poor grip on a golf club is among the most prevalent problems plaguing weekend players. It never ceases to amaze me how the majority of golfers can spend their golfing lives without properly gripping a club. Probably two out of every one hundred golfers actually hold a club correctly.

If you happen to be one of the 2 percent who do, then you already have this first fundamental licked. But more likely you aren't, so I urge you to pay close attention to this chapter.

First, don't worry if your grip needs work. You're far from being alone. Second, make up your mind that you're going to develop a good grip and stick with it. It will be difficult at first because the correct grip won't feel natural. At first, it's natural to grip a golf club the same way you grip a baseball bat, or a broom, or a suitcase handle, but it's *wrong*. If anything, the golf grip resembles two backhand grips on a tennis racquet.

Like the good backhand tennis grip, the correct golf grip puts part of the palms of both hands on the *top* of the club instead of facing each other on the sides. This position allows both hands to work as a unit throughout the swing. Although there are several types of golf grip, this primary premise is present in all of them and is essential to achieving a solid impact.

I use the type of grip called the overlapping, or Vardon, grip, named after the great turn-of-the-century English champion Harry Vardon. I started out holding the club with the Vardon grip and I've always felt very comfortable with it.

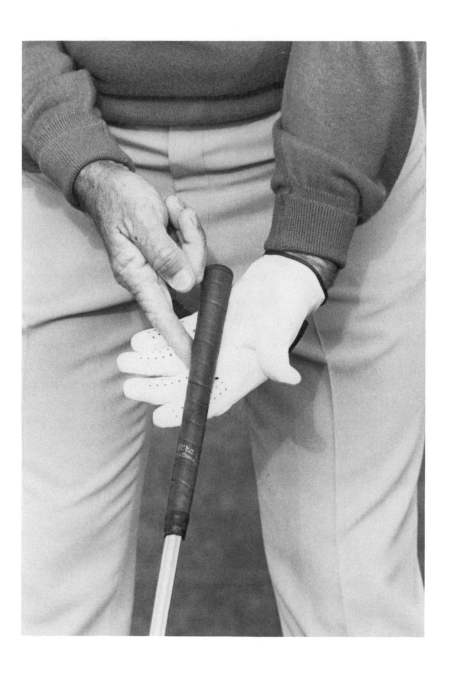

Open the left hand and lay the club diagonally across the palm.

HOW TO TAKE THE GRIP

In taking the Vardon grip, start with your left hand. Open it and lay the club diagonally across your left palm so that the grip of the club runs right across the middle section of your index finger and the butt of the grip ends just to the right of the corner of the heel pad of your hand. The club is in the right position if you are able to wrap the heel pad and part of your palm over the top of the club so that your thumb points straight down the shaft.

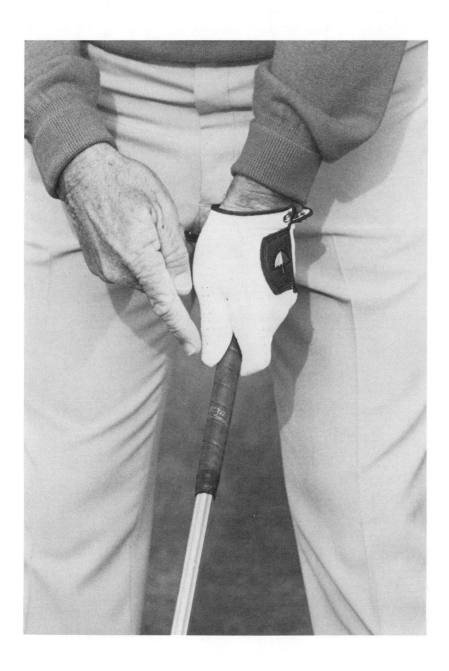

Wrap the heel pad and part of the palm over the top so the thumb points straight down the shaft.

Feel strange? If it does, guard against letting the heel pad slide to the left side, the way it would on a baseball bat. Keep it anchored *on top* of the club, again like a backhand grip in tennis. As in tennis, the backhand grip feels unnatural until you master it. Once you have, you'll wonder how you ever held the club in any other way.

Now for your right hand. First, place it on the club below your left hand, covering the left thumb with the pocket located below the base of your right thumb. Second, wrap your fingers around and underneath the grip, overlapping the little finger of your right hand into the valley formed by the index and forefinger of your left hand.

You now have the right grip.

The back of the left hand should face the target.

The fingers should be snug together with no gaps between them.

Wrap the fingers of the right hand underneath the grip, covering the left thumb with the pocket below the base of the right thumb.

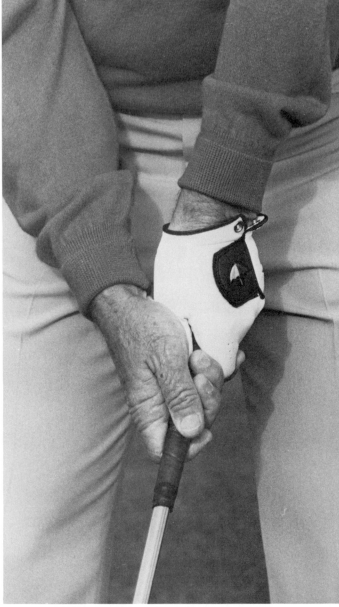

Both hands should be rotated toward each other toward the top of the club so the palms are pressing downward from the twelve o'clock position.

Be sure the hands fit firmly together so they function as a unit during the swing.

There are a couple of things I'd like you to take special note of. First, notice you're holding the club mainly with the last three fingers of your left hand and the middle two fingers of your right hand. The bottom finger pads of these fingers (the pads closest to the palms) are all *under* the grip, allowing the club to rest snugly on them and be cradled by the fingers.

The club should be cradled in the fingers, resting snugly on the bottom pads of each one.

The last three fingers on the left hand do most of the work in holding the club.

Let the middle two fingers of the right hand exert the most pressure.

Second, notice from the top of the grip how both hands are rotated toward each other toward the top of the club, so that both palms are pressing downward from the twelve o'clock position. *The grip of the club is being balanced between the palms pressing down from above and the fingers pressing up from below.*

The Vardon Grip: Overlap the little finger of the right hand into the valley formed by the index and forefinger of the left hand.

The Interlocking Grip: Interweave the index finger of the left hand with the little finger of the right.

The Ten-Finger, or Baseball, Grip: Place all ten fingers on the club, with the left index finger resting snugly against the little finger of the right hand.

If overlapping the little finger of the right hand onto the left feels too uncomfortable, try one of the other two popular grip variations: the interlocking grip, which unites the hands by interweaving the index finger of the left hand with the little finger of the right; or the ten-finger grip (also known as the baseball grip), which places all ten fingers on the club, with the left index finger lying snugly *against* the little finger of the right hand.

Choose whichever type of grip you prefer or feels best and most natural, provided you position your hands with your palms on top of the club.

WEAK, NEUTRAL, AND STRONG POSITIONS

Grip position pertains to how far your hands are turned over on the club. This is extremely important in squaring the clubface to the ball at impact. If your hands do not return to the same position at impact as they were at address, the clubface won't be square, and you won't get straight shots.

To determine the position of your hands, simply look at the "V" formed by the thumb and first finger of your left hand after it's been positioned on the club. If the "V" points to your chin, you have a *weak* grip. If it points to your right shoulder, your grip is *neutral*. If it points past your right shoulder, you have a *strong* grip.

I recommend that you start out in a neutral grip position and check the direction of your shots. If they curve from left to right, you aren't squaring the clubface at impact. Try turning *both* hands gradually to the right toward a stronger grip position until your shots start going straight.

If, with a neutral grip, your shots are curving from right to left, you're closing the clubface at impact and need to weaken your grip. Gradually turn *both* hands to the left until your shots straighten out.

Weaker players often benefit from a stronger grip position because it puts the thumbs behind the shaft on the downswing, giving them greater leverage on the downswing, and allowing a stronger release of the hands through the hitting zone.

Stronger players, who have stronger hands, may find a weaker grip position more desirable, since they usually have little trouble building clubhead speed or releasing the hands.

Experiment with your grip positions to find the one that suits you best.

GETTING THE PROPER WRIST ACTION

Gripping the golf club properly stabilizes the wrists, allowing them to cock automatically during the swing in a controlled fashion. Unlike baseball, where the wrists break more during a swing of the bat because the palms face each other in the grip, too much wrist movement is not desirable in golf. Sloppy wrists lead to a poor swing path and preclude putting the clubface squarely on the ball. This results in a lot of errant shots.

In the golf swing, the hands and shoulders do more work than the wrists. This is directly opposed to the baseball bat swing, where quick, strong wrist action is important to good hitting. When you stop to think about it this makes a lot of sense. In golf, the contact with the ball must be so much more precise because accuracy is so important.

In a baseball park, you can hit the ball to different areas and still get good results. You can hit it straight ahead to center field, to left field, or to right field; on the ground or through the air; long or short.

To score well on the golf course, however, you have to be precise, both in the distance and direction you hit the ball. You have to make contact squarely on the clubface every time to get it airborne on a desired trajectory. Because so much more precision is required in golf, there's little room for error with the wrists. Remember, the correct grip controls the wrists. It prevents them from making any excess movement, which ruins ball control.

The correct grip probably will feel very awkward at first. That's natural and is a clear indicator that your old one was far different and, therefore, far from good. I really can't emphasize strongly enough how important it is to stick with it. It won't take long to get used to, and once you have, you'll wonder how you ever held the club any other way.

The correct grip will feel even better once you start consistently hitting the ball longer and straighter on a permanent basis.

That's a promise.

2
The Address

Now that you have the proper grip to work with, the second of the Five Fundamentals you should tackle is the address. Address is the position a golfer puts his body in before making a swing. The address "sets the table," so to speak, for a good swing motion to occur. It puts the parts of the body that are crucial to the swing—the head, shoulders, hands, hips, legs, and feet—where they should be to get a good swing started.

The address is a ready position, much like a baseball batter waiting for a pitch to come in or a tennis player waiting for a serve. The feeling is halfway between relaxation and tension, as you prepare to make a fluid yet controlled swing of the club through the ball.

Two combined elements make up the address position: posture and alignment. Let's take posture first.

POSTURE

Posture involves how you stand in reference to the ball, and how you distribute your body weight.

Starting without a club, try getting into the right posture position. First, spread your feet to about shoulder width, making sure both feet are flat on the ground. Distribute your weight evenly between the insides of both and evenly between the balls and heels. Flex your knees slightly and bend slightly forward at the waist. Keep your back straight and extend your derrière backward so that your arms hang loosely, straight down.

You should feel firmly planted on the ground. You should be so stable that were someone to push you from any direction, you couldn't be pushed off balance. In fact, that's an excellent way to find out whether or not your posture *is* correct.

Good posture at address is crucial to making a good swing. Flex the knees slightly, bend forward at the waist, keeping the back straight and letting your arms hang down loosely.

ALIGNMENT

Now that you're balanced, you're ready to go on to alignment. Whereas posture concerned the up and down position of the body, in other words, from head to toe, alignment concerns how the horizontal lines of the body—shoulders, hips, knees, feet—square up at address.

Everything should be square, or parallel, to the imaginary target line, which runs from the ball straight to the target. The

In learning the proper address, it's best to start in a square position, lining up the feet, hips, and shoulders parallel to the target line.

idea is similar to the way a basketball player squares up to the hoop or a bowler squares his shoulders to the lane.

You're ready to take your club in hand and put it all together. Take a driver and assume your newly learned grip. Spread your feet and distribute your weight evenly from side to side, front to back. Next, flex your knees slightly and bend forward at the waist so the arms dangle freely without reaching forward, the hands positioned a little ahead of the clubhead. The ball should be opposite your left heel, where you'll position it with every club. Pick out an imaginary target and check that your hips, shoulders, and feet are parallel to it. Also check that the clubface is square to it.

Do you feel relaxed and ready? Then congratulations! You've achieved the proper address. You're now in the best position you can be to make a proper swing at the ball.

The importance of a good address cannot be overestimated. Good posture assures a good weight shift for power and a sound swing plane. Good alignment helps guarantee a sound swing path for solid, straight shots. But you won't have to worry about any of this, for when a good address position is combined with the other four fundamentals, the swing path and swing plane will take care of themselves. You'll know when you're right because you'll be hitting the ball straight and far.

3
The Takeaway

Learning the Five Fundamentals allows every golfer to naturally develop his own distinctive, though effective, swing.

The takeaway is one of the Five Fundamentals that most directly involves the actual motion of the swing. It is the very start of the backswing, more specifically, it is the first couple of feet that the club travels away from the ball.

The takeaway is the most crucial part of the entire golf swing. If your takeaway is good, you *can't help* but make a sound swing. The rest of the backswing and downswing will fall into place. It's that easy.

START IN ONE PIECE

Even simpler is how to go about making a good takeaway. The key is to take the club back in an even, one-piece motion so that the straight line formed from the clubhead to the top of the left shoulder remains unbroken for the first two feet the club travels away from the ball.

This doesn't mean keeping your arms and wrists stiff, just firm, without allowing your wrists to break. Once you've reached the end of the takeaway, let your arms take their natural course. Don't even think about wrist cock, body rotation, clubhead path, or swing plane. These things will happen naturally. If you keep your right side relaxed while going back and your left relatively firm, your right arm will automatically fold and point to the ground. Allow this to happen, and you'll naturally swing on a good plane and set the club in a good solid position at the top, with the club shaft parallel to the target line.

Make the takeaway a one-piece motion, maintaining the straight line that's formed from the clubhead to the left shoulder as you push the clubhead straight away from the ball.

You automatically will make a good backswing if you get into the proper address position and make a good takeaway.

Halfway back, the weight shifts to the inside of the right foot; the arms and hands roll over and naturally take an inside course, bringing the club back on a solid, slightly inside path.

At the top, the right elbow has folded under and points to the ground, the shoulders have made a good turn, and the arms and hands have set the club in a good position at the top.

If you make a good backswing, the downswing will result almost automatically. Shift your weight left and let the shoulders and arms unwind and deliver the clubhead squarely to the ball.

Swing the arms *through* the ball, keeping the club moving well through the hitting zone and the body behind the ball.

A good finish will naturally result from a good downswing: the weight will be on the left foot, chest pointing left of the target and the hands high over the left shoulder.

One thing that always ruins the chances of making a good takeaway is starting the swing with a quick, jerky motion. I don't believe a player's swing has to be rhythmic to be effective, so long as he has the correct fundamentals. The best way to ensure making a solid takeaway is to work on starting it *smoothly* and *evenly*.

Front view with a 5-iron.

Again, note the one-piece action of the left side and the low, straight path of the clubhead away from the ball.

With a one-piece takeaway, you can't help but turn your shoulders and hips properly and shift your weight correctly so that most of it is on the inside of your right foot at the top of the backswing.

Keeping the clubhead low on the takeaway helps create a good extension of the hands away from the ball, creating a wide swing arc that results in added power.

At the top, the weight has moved to the right side but my right knee remains flexed. My left arm is relatively straight, and my wrists have cocked fully.

Halfway down, my shoulders are unwinding, pulling my arms and hands with them. My wrists are uncocking naturally, and my knees are "pointing" to the left in the direction of the weight shift, indicating good lower body action.

The degree of body turn depends on flexibility, body type, strength, and coordination. It obviously will be different for a lot of golfers. This is part of what makes a good swing by one person look different from a good swing by another.

Remember to take the club back as far as you can *without* straining or moving your head.

At impact, a relatively straight line is formed from the clubhead to my left shoulder. My upper body stays well behind the ball as my hands square the clubface to it. Most of my weight has been transferred to the left side.

There's a natural limitation to everyone's swing and it's important not to try to force it past that. Otherwise, you'll be adding errors to your natural motion.

Unfortunately, more than a few amateurs are guilty of this pushing, which comes from trying to imitate professional players. I have often been cited as having a very big shoulder turn.

My turn was never anything that I *consciously* developed. It's a natural part of *my* swing, not something I think about when I hit the ball.

That's why you should figure out the amount of turn that's right for *you* and stick with it. If your body is thick, or if your body lacks suppleness, you simply will never be able to turn your shoulders as far as a professional player does; you just aren't built for it. Therefore, it's senseless to try. It will only lead to a loss of clubhead control and a sacrifice of accuracy.

Remember, power in golf is valuable only if you can control it consistently. If you can't, it will cause you more harm than good.

TRY THIS EXPERIMENT

The difference in distance produced by a full swing and a three-quarter swing actually is very small. Surprised? Through some experimentation on my own, I've found that I hit the ball only about 10 percent farther with a full swing than with a three-quarter swing. So if you are guilty of trying to go beyond the normal boundary that your body has set for you in a quest for more power, you are sacrificing a lot of control for what will prove to be a marginal increase in distance.

Try this experiment for yourself. Seeing is believing.

Recreational golfers too often forget that the player who hits the ball in the fairway usually has little trouble outscoring a longer hitting opponent who is all over the lot. Look at the statistics kept on the Tour pros. Those who top the accuracy lists are also doing very well on the money list. That is not always true for those pros who make up the top ten on the driving distance list.

Now that we've covered the third fundamental, you can see that if you make the effort to ingrain the one-piece takeaway, the rest of your body will follow suit. You'll be well on your way to playing great golf.

4
The Still Head

Keep your head still. It sounds like a tired cliché, but actually it's one of the most important of the Five Fundamentals of the golf swing.

One of the traits that I have been most famous for throughout my career has been my ability to maintain a still head position while hitting the ball. Although certain parts of my swing have been talked about over the years as not being the accepted way, nearly all of the critics have agreed that my head position was always good. No matter how hard I swung at the ball, I kept my head very still.

Keeping your head still during the swing is certainly easier said than done, a statement I make from experience. I have worked harder to master this than all of the other fundamentals put together. When I was six years old, my father told me to go ahead and hit the ball as hard as I wanted to, *so long as I kept my head still.* I've been working at it ever since.

When I say still, I mean exactly that, no movement upward, downward, or side to side allowed. Any head movement minimizes your chances of making square, solid contact and reduces your chances of hitting the ball straight and with power.

The lines on this photograph indicate the position of my head at the start of the swing.

Keeping the head in a relatively still position keeps the hub of the swing steady, ensuring that the swing circle stays on one consistent plane throughout the entire motion.

Maintaining a still head almost guarantees a solid delivery of the clubhead to the back of the ball every time. You can see by the lines that my head is in almost the same position at impact as when I started the swing.

You can see by the lines that my head stays still until well after impact.

As I extend my arms through the hitting zone, my head maintains its position.

The head releases and rises automatically as the weight moves to the outside of the left foot in the finish.

The reason is very simple: Imagine your swing is a circle, with your head at the center and the ball a point at the very bottom. When the center of the circle moves, so does the circle. If the circle moves, the clubhead will no longer pass squarely through the point at the bottom.

There *is* a difference, though, between keeping your head still and keeping your eye on the ball. Take your address position and try intentionally moving your head around while watching the ball. You'll see what I mean. It's possible to move your head two feet in any direction while keeping the ball in sight. So while you should keep your eyes focused on the ball, realize that it's not the same as keeping your head still.

I can't tell you any secrets about how to keep your head still, only that it requires practice and discipline. Most players keep it in a static position from takeaway to impact, when the force of the follow-through finally pulls it up along with the upper body.

Once you can keep your head steady, you'll be ready to do what Pap told me years ago, hit it as hard as you want!

5
Acceleration

The final of the Five Fundamentals is different from the other four because it doesn't directly involve the physical positioning or movement of a part or parts of the body before or during the swing. It does affect the type of follow-through you make. The fifth fundamental is acceleration, the constantly increasing speed at which the clubhead must be moving through impact to hit the ball crisply and with power.

Because the follow-through is basically the product of a proper downswing motion, it's usually a reliable indicator of the kind of acceleration you're putting into the ball. If your follow-through isn't winning any prizes, then you probably aren't accelerating the way you should through the hitting zone. If you were, the force of the club swinging freely would be enough to carry you into a good, full finish. Your hands should be high over your left shoulder, most of your weight should be on the outside of your left heel, and your chest should be pointing to the left of the target.

DECELERATION EQUALS MISSED SHOTS

One of the main causes of poor shotmaking is decelerating the club into the ball, whether on a drive, a pitch, or a putt. Think about the last time you stood on the tee of a par three undecided over which club to use, and opted to swing easy with the stronger one. I doubt if your tentative downswing put your ball on the green.

Deceleration usually is caused by fear, fear of going over the green; fear of driving into trouble; fear of dumping the ball in the sand when forced to pitch over a bunker; and fear of knocking a slippery downhill putt ten feet past the cup. Such fears cause both physical and mental tension within you so that you try to steer the ball instead of hitting through it with a brisk, aggressive stroke.

Those who have seen me play know that I always tend to take a pretty healthy cut at the ball—far from tentative. I'm not saying that you have to swing as hard as I do. I am saying that the speed you swing the clubhead has to increase as you hit through the ball to hit good golf shots. *You must* accelerate.

I don't think swing tempo is very important. Everyone swings at a pace that's consistent with his individual personality. Energetic people tend to swing fast. They naturally start their downswing fast and reach impact only slightly faster. Relaxed people usually are comfortable at an easier pace. They naturally build speed in a slow, smooth manner, with a crescendo of power. However, if both types of golfer accelerate into the ball on the downswing and have the other four fundamentals down pat, they'll hit the ball well.

Acceleration is easiest to achieve when the transition between the backswing and downswing is smooth. Whatever your natural body turn is, think of your hands as coasting to a stop at the top and as smoothly changing directions before picking up speed.

Remember, whenever you're in a tight situation where the margin for error on the shot is very small, make clubhead acceleration your top priority.

Say you have a short pitch over a deep bunker to a tight pin position. The fear of dumping the ball into the bunker promotes a tension that leads to deceleration on the downstroke. The result? Your fear is realized. In such a situation, make sure you accelerate into the ball on the downswing.

Doing this alone will probably knock three strokes off your average score right off the bat.

Summary

The Grip
The Address
The Takeaway
The Still Head
Acceleration

These are the Five Fundamentals. When put together, they produce an effective golf swing for almost anyone. Each fundamental carries equal weight and plays a crucial role in hitting successful shots. The absence of one will create a serious chink in anyone's golfing armor. So pay strict attention to incorporating each of them into your normal swing motion.

Certain fundamentals may need more attention than others, depending upon the individual. Take the time to learn each, and turn a deaf ear to any other advice that may come your way. That kind of help, however well meaning, is best ignored. Instead, stick to this game plan and the principles of the Five Fundamentals. They are the only help you'll ever need.

PART II

USING
THE
INDIVIDUAL
CLUBS

A QUICK RUN THROUGH THE BAG

Now that we have been through, and you understand, the fundamentals of a good swing, let's see how they apply to the different clubs—the short, medium, and long irons; the fairway woods and the driver.

Golfers often complain that they hit the short irons well but the longer ones poorly, or vice versa. What they don't realize is that every club varies in both clubface loft and shaft length and that they must vary the angle of attack on the ball to make the best possible contact with each. Generally, the less lofted the club, the shallower the angle of attack should be. Conversely, the more lofted the club, the more descending the angle should be.

The best way to change the angle of attack is to adjust your stance at address.

With the driver and fairway woods, your stance should be fairly wide and square to accommodate the long, sweeping, swing motion required to hit these clubs well. But as you go

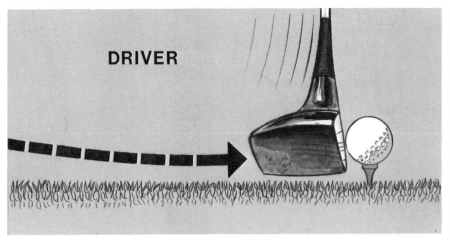

DRIVER

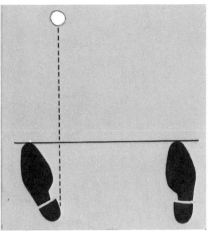

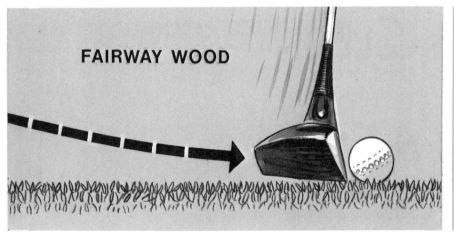

FAIRWAY WOOD

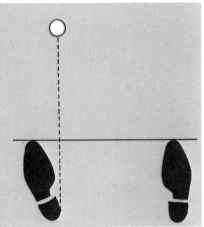

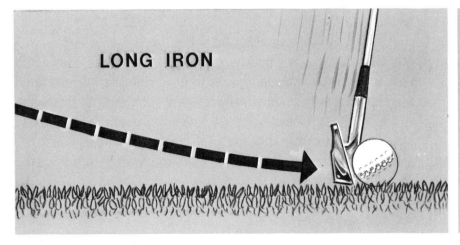

LONG IRON

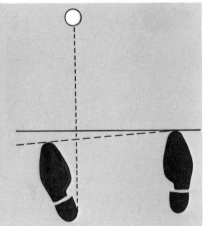

Angles of attack for various clubs.

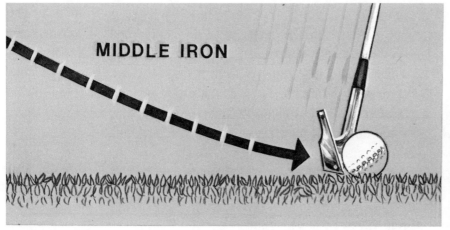

MIDDLE IRON

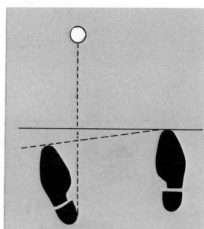

SHORT IRON

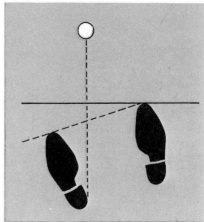

down through the bag, to the long, middle, and short irons, you should progressively narrow and open your stance to set up the increasingly descending downswing angles required. You'll find that positioning your feet in relation to the length of the shaft—open and narrow for shorter ones; wide and more square for longer ones—feels extremely natural and is very easy to get used to.

Hitting the medium and short irons with a more descending blow is important in giving the maximum amount of backspin to the shot. One of the questions I'm most often asked when I give an instruction clinic is, "How do you put backspin on the ball? Or how do you make it back up?"

Let me assure you that even though your ball may not dance when you hit a 9-iron onto a green the way you've seen the pros do, you *are* getting some backspin on your ball. The loft on the clubface assures it. Your shots lack action because they don't spin nearly as much as the professionals' shots do. They usually lose most of their spin on the first bounce. Every club puts some degree of backspin on the ball, even the relatively straight-faced driver. In fact, every ball *has* to have some spin on it just to get up into the air at all.

THE SECRET OF BACKSPIN

The *amount* of backspin put on a particular shot depends upon a number of factors.

As far as how you swing and make contact with the ball goes, it is the difference between the angle of attack on the downswing and the angle of the clubface that directly influence how much the ball will spin. The steeper the downswing angle and the more lofted the club, the more backspin is produced; the shallower the downswing angle, the less backspin is produced. That explains why your stance should get increasingly opened to create a more descending downswing blow as the clubs get higher.

It also explains the importance of keeping your hands in good position—just slightly ahead of the ball—at impact, to strike the shot with the true loft of the clubface.

Also crucial to putting good backspin on the ball is the particular playing conditions of the shot.

First, you must have a lie that allows an absolutely clean club-to-ball contact. Anything getting in between this contact, even a few, tiny blades of grass or a bit of moisture if the ground is wet, reduces greatly the amount of backspin you will get.

Second, the condition of the green has to be just right to make the ball "suck back." If it's sloping away from you, *no one* could make the ball back up going uphill. The surface of the green has to be either flat or sloping toward you.

The firmness of the surface of the green also is a factor. A well-spun shot will bite a lot more into a soft surface than a hard one.

Finally, wind direction makes a difference in the amount of spin you'll get on a shot. If it's coming toward you, you'll get more spin; if it's at your back, you will get less spin.

I'll explain exactly how stance adjustments help you achieve the correct downswing angle in the next section on the individual clubs. Before I do, however, I'd like to emphasize that it's essential to make these changes if you want to hit all the clubs well, not just some of them.

Your stance should be the *only* thing that changes when you hit the different clubs. Everything else—grip, address, takeaway, head position, and acceleration into the ball—should remain the same on *every* swing with *every* club. This is very important.

With this last thought firmly in mind, let's look at the individual clubs in more detail.

6
The Clubs

SHORT IRONS

The short irons—7-, 8-, 9-, pitching wedge, and sand wedge—
are the weekend players' most valuable scoring clubs, next to
the putter. Their function is accuracy, not distance. This is best
illustrated by their greater loft for hitting high, soft landing
shots, and their shorter shafts for making short, controlled
swings.

To play the short irons well, you must contact the ball with
a descending blow on a steep downswing path, striking first the
ball then the ground. This is the opposite of the shallower,
more sweeping motion required to hit the lower, straighter-
faced clubs, such as a driver.

The key to making a good descending blow with the short
irons is to play them with an *open* stance.

Getting into an open stance is fairly simple. First, set up
squarely to the ball. Then pull your left foot back about two
inches, as if you were aiming at an object slightly left of your
intended target. Be sure that your clubface remains square to
the target line, that your entire body is aligned left and that
your hips and shoulders are parallel to the line set by your feet.

Assume your address position, with the ball opposite your
left heel, letting the length of the shaft dictate how far you stand
from the ball. Your feet should be spread about twelve inches
apart in a fairly narrow stance. Swing normally along the line
set by your body.

Opening your stance won't change your swing, but it will
shift the angle on which the club approaches the ball. The
clubhead will come in on a steeper, more sharply descending
path on the ball and then into the turf. From there, the loft on

the clubface will get the ball up into the air. The shortness of the clubshaft also helps you swing the club on a steeper path. Its length naturally inhibits a long, low takeaway and automatically forces a slightly sharper arc.

The Premium Is on Accuracy

A final thought on short irons: *don't force them*. Many players make their selection of these clubs into an ego-trip. They try to swing for a 130-yard shot with a wedge when the distance calls for a 7- or 8-iron. As a result, they may play the hole with a drive and a wedge but conveniently forget to tell you that their second shot finished in the rough or in a bunker.

A better idea is to do what we pros do and play well within yourself with these clubs. You'll be more accurate and you'll probably have more short birdie putts coming up in your game.

PLAYER'S WINNING 9-IRON AT THE '72 PGA

One of the greatest short iron shots ever hit in a major championship had to be Gary Player's 9-iron on the sixteenth hole of the final round of the 1972 PGA Championship held at Oakland Hills Country Club in Birmingham, Michigan.

Tied with Jim Jamieson, who was playing two holes ahead of him, Player pushed his drive off the sixteenth tee, a 408 yard par four that doglegs sharply to the right around a lake that hugs the right side of the green.

His ball finished in the rough 150 yards from the green behind a large willow tree. After sizing up the shot carefully, he elected to play over the tree instead of trying to fade the ball around it, though a 9-iron was the lowest club he could use while still making sure of getting the ball high enough to clear the willow.

Tearing into the shot, it rose quickly and cleanly cleared the tree. From there Gary lost sight of it; his vision blocked by the willow's branches. He quickly lay down on the ground to look under them and spied the ball lying just four feet from the pin. His birdie putt there and ensuing pars on seventeen and eighteen gave him a two stroke victory and his second PGA title.

MIDDLE IRONS

The friendliest clubs in the bags of most weekend players are the middle irons—the 4-, 5-, and 6-. Why? Because they are easy clubs to hit. The loft of their faces lies between the short irons and long irons, and so they are neither extremely straight-faced nor extremely laid back. Their shafts, too, have a more comfortable length, neither long nor short.

The type of swing path required to hit successful middle iron shots is in between the fairly steep path needed to hit the short irons and the shallower path needed to hit the long irons.

The setup position for the middle irons is virtually the same as for the short irons, with two exceptions.

First your address position will be a little less open. This will flatten out your downswing path slightly, and you will make a slightly less descending blow. Pull your left foot back about 1 to 1½ inches from the square position. Do likewise with your hips and shoulders.

Second, widen your stance a little more than with the short irons. The longer shafts on these clubs and the squarer stance allow you to take a longer swing. Therefore, you'll need

TWO ACES IN TWO DAYS

Not just one but two 5-iron shots that I've made stand out in my mind, because they were indeed "career" shots. Both came on the same hole of the same course in the same tournament: It happened during the inaugural Chrysler Cup at the Tournament Players Course at Avenel in suburban Washington, D.C., in September 1986. The hole was the third, a par three.

The first occurred during a Tuesday pro-am when the hole measured 187 yards. My shot landed about ten feet short of the hole, bounced a couple of times, hit the base of the pin, and dropped in for an ace. Needless to say, it's always a thrill to score a hole-in-one, even for a professional. It was a shot I knew I'd have on my mind for a while.

But on the next day came another pro-am and, incredibly, another hole-in-one, again on the third hole. This time it measured 182 yards, and again I took out my 5-iron. The shot covered the flag the entire way, and to my disbelief, as well as that of about a hundred onlookers around the green, the ball dove into the hole on the fly with a loud clank against the pin.

Two aces in two days. Sometimes I still can't believe it!

to have your feet spread a little farther apart to maintain stability and balance throughout your swing.

Like the short irons, the middle irons are accuracy clubs and are to be swung in a controlled manner. The key to being successful with them is to hit them where you're aiming, *not* the fact that you can hit your 5-iron fifteen yards farther than the average guy. Chances are that average guy is going to be a lot more accurate than you are, if you're straining for every bit of distance you can get.

Follow the above setup steps and swing in control. As a result, you'll probably make your friendly middle irons even more friendly.

LONG IRONS

Long irons are not the easiest clubs for most weekend players to hit well. In fact, most golfers, professionals and amateurs alike, would agree that the long irons are the clubs that most differentiate those who play golf for a living and those who play it for fun.

What makes long irons so difficult to hit? Well, for one, their limited loft. Obviously, the 1-, 2-, and 3-irons carry less loft than the middle and short irons. So, it's tougher to get the ball up into the air because there's less margin for error. You can hit a 6-iron or 9-iron and "not get it all," but still get the ball airborne and come up with a reasonable shot. However, anything less than square contact with one of the longer irons usually results in a grounded ball.

Don't think that only professional players have the talent to hit the longer irons. If you have your fundamentals down, there's no reason why you can't hit them too. The key in hitting long irons well is to swing through the ball with a more sweeping motion and make contact with the ball first.

To do this, simply set up to the shot with a slightly open stance. Pull your left foot back just one-half to one inch from square and widen your stance a bit, so you can maintain your balance throughout the longer swing that comes with the greater shaft lengths of the long irons.

Swing normally, trusting the loft of the clubface to get the ball airborne. It doesn't look like much, I know, but there's plenty there to get the ball up. You just have to strike it squarely. Concentrate on accelerating the clubhead *through* the ball with good speed, don't punch at it.

NICKLAUS AND HIS 1-IRON

One of the finest long-iron shots I've ever witnessed was hit by Jack Nicklaus on the eighteenth hole of the final round of the 1967 U.S. Open at Baltusrol Golf Club in Springfield, New Jersey.

Jack and I had started the last round tied for second place with Billy Casper, a stroke behind Marty Fleckman. As Fleckman and Casper faded, the battle came down to Nicklaus and me, and by the final tee Jack had built up a four-stroke lead. Still, anything could happen.

The finishing hole at Baltusrol is a long par five of 542 yards that's reachable with two big shots. My drive was perfect: long and straight, whereas Jack pushed his 1-iron into the right rough. Playing safe with an 8-iron on the second shot, he mishit the ball and moved it about fifty yards toward the hole. Meanwhile, I played my second shot with a 3-wood into a good position to the right of the plateau green.

For his third shot, Jack decided against playing safe. Taking the 1-iron again, he hit a long, high fade into a light breeze. It carried over a bunker, faded to a gentle landing barely short of the green and ran up to within twenty-two feet of the hole, icing his victory.

You don't have to swing the long irons any harder than the other clubs. You may be a hard swinger by nature, that's fine, but no matter what your swing tempo is, keep it the same with every club—especially with the long irons.

Swing at your regular tempo, and you have a far better chance of making square contact with good clubhead speed. Both factors are crucial, of course, to hitting every club well, but they're especially important to hitting the long irons. Don't make the mistake of trying to add something extra and sacrifice your control. You don't have to. Simply trust the loft of the club and swing freely through the ball. Your trust will be rewarded.

The 1-iron

If you happen to be pretty proficient with the long irons, you may want to try a 1-iron, a club that combines excellent distance with the control of an iron.

Not usually included with most standard sets, the 1-iron is a club that few players, most of them professionals, have the ability to hit well. Its small amount of loft (17 degrees) demands exceptional clubhead speed to have any success with it.

If you think you might be able to handle a 1-iron, ask your club pro to let you borrow one to try on the practice tee. Besides delivering excellent distance from the fairway, it's a great club for control off the tee when hitting to a tight fairway or for keeping the ball low when conditions are windy.

FAIRWAY WOODS

The fairway woods can be tremendous assets to the player who hits them well, affording the maximum distance to shots played off the fairway. Proficiency with these clubs—the 3-, 4-, and 5-woods—can make the greens of many par fives reachable in two shots for some players while helping shorter hitters reach the greens of many long par fours with two shots as well.

Handicap players often feel more comfortable with the fairway woods than long irons for several reasons. First, the faces of the woods are more lofted and less intimidating than the straighter faces of the long irons. Second, the shafts are longer, supplying a wider arc for more clubhead speed. Third, they are lighter in weight than the long irons, which also helps build clubhead speed. Fourth, the large head of the wood often gives the player a positive feeling that he'll hit the ball more solidly.

3-WOOD TO THE STICK

Probably the finest fairway wood shot I've ever struck came in a losing effort at the 1968 PGA Championship at Pecan Valley Country Club in San Antonio, Texas. With one hole left to play, I needed a birdie to tie Julius Boros, who was playing in the group behind me.

The finishing hole is a 470-yard par four that dog-legs, or bends, right. A creek crosses the fairway about 245 yards out, forcing the player to lay up on his drive and hit a long iron into the elevated green.

My drive wasn't a good one, though. It hooked left and finished in heavy rough about 230 yards from the green. Figuring Boros would finish with a par, I took a 3-wood and went for the green. With a lashing swing, the clubhead slid hard through the high grass, propelling the ball out on a low, slightly hooking path that landed just short of the green and rolled up to the flag. It struck the stick and ricocheted past, stopping eight feet away.

It wasn't to be. I expected my putt to break a fraction of an inch, but it stayed straight and hung on the lip for a tap-in par. Behind me, Boros missed the green with his second shot, but got up and down for the win.

Playing the fairway woods requires a similar swing to that used with the long irons—a sweeping motion of the clubhead through the ball on a very shallow downswing path.

To play a fairway wood shot, set up to the ball in a square stance, with both of your feet aligned parallel to the target line, along with your hips and shoulders. Aligning yourself this way allows you to get the shallowest arc possible on your downswing. Your objective is to hit the ball first while the club is traveling at the very bottom of the swing arc. Hitting down on the ball with a descending blow results in a pop-up. Your feet should be a little wider apart than with the long irons.

Fairway woods are best used from good lies, although the better and more confident you become with them, the more you can experiment with using them from a variety of lies.

One final note about the fairway woods. Many weekend players opt to take their 2-irons out of their bags and replace them with 5-woods, which, besides being easier to hit, provide a higher, softer-landing trajectory. Club manufacturers also have responded to this by producing even more lofted woods, like the 6- and 7-. Such clubs can be excellent alternatives for many players, especially women and seniors, who are often physically unable to generate the clubhead speed necessary to hit their long irons well. Those of you who have this problem should seriously consider making this trade.

THE DRIVER

We've finally reached my favorite club, the driver. For an aggressive player like me, the driver is the most fun club in the bag. It really gives me a chance to let out the shaft and get the most yardage from my swing. Few things compare with catching the ball on the screws and watching it sail straight and hard 275 yards down the fairway.

More importantly, a good drive puts you in a position to make your approach to the green of a par four or gives you a chance to try to get home in two on a par five. Work hard at becoming a good driver because it will pay tremendous dividends by increasing your chances of hitting greens in regulation.

The key to hitting a driver well is to swing on a very shallow swing arc, making contact with the ball while the clubhead is traveling at the very bottom of the arc. This enables

Set up square, with the ball positioned opposite your left heel, teed high enough to make it easy to sweep it toward your target.

the clubface to drive the ball directly toward the target. To best do this, set up to the ball with a square stance. Your feet, hips, and shoulders should be positioned square to the target line. Set your feet fractionally wider apart than with the fairway woods, about shoulder width apart is good.

Position the ball off your left heel, teed high enough so that you'll have no trouble sweeping it off at the bottom of your swing arc. Some golfers play the ball farther up off the instep or even off the toe, but that encourages catching the ball slightly on the upswing. I find it's better to get it right at the bottom of your swing and drive the ball straight to the target.

For my drives, I tee the ball about an inch off the ground. Teeing it lower forces too descending a blow, which pops the ball up and costs you a lot of distance. Take care in how you tee the ball, because it's usually the only time you can be sure the lie is perfect on a full-swing shot.

Controlled Power

I don't think there's a golfer alive who doesn't get a certain amount of satisfaction out of hitting the long ball. Let's face the facts though, power off the tee, or anywhere else in golf, isn't worth a darn thing unless it's *controlled* power.

A good drive should place your ball in the best position possible to approach the green of a par four or make a good second shot on a par five. If it doesn't, then your scoring is going to suffer. You could be the best iron player in the world, but if you're consistently using them from the rough, fairway bunkers, or the woods, your scoring will undoubtedly suffer. That's why it's vitally important to be accurate as well as powerful with your number one wood.

The Key to Accurate Driving

There's no big secret to driving a golf ball accurately. Just apply the Five Fundamentals to every swing off the tee and see how often you go astray.

Unfortunately, in their quest for added distance, most weekend players force errors into their swings that result in a lot of misguided shots. The most common fault I see among amateurs trying to pound the ball is their head movement. In trying to reach back for something extra, or in an effort to give it all they've got on the downswing, they move their heads,

A BIG OPENING DRIVE

Going into the final round of the 1960 U.S. Open at Cherry Hills Country Club in Denver, Colorado, I trailed the leader Mike Souchak, by seven shots. But I had a hunch I still could win if I started strong and got the ball rolling early.

The first hole, a relatively short par four with an elevated tee, measured 346 yards, which I felt was driveable, especially in the thin air of the "Mile High" City, where golf shots typically go about 10 percent farther than they do at sea level. There was, however, a patch of heavy rough that had been allowed to grow up about sixty yards in front of the green to discourage long hitters from making the attempt.

Deciding to risk it for the sake of making a big start, I hit the opening driver with everything I had and got every bit of the ball—a draw that ran right through that patch of rough and up into the heart of the green, finishing twenty feet from the cup. That drive led to the first of six birdies on the front nine and a finishing 65—good for a two-stroke victory.

which shifts their swing center. The result is poor contact with the ball.

Remember what my father told me? "Hit it as hard as you want—*just don't move your head.*" Of all the clubs discussed, this applies especially to the driver, because you tend to take such a big rip at it. Also, a mishit, or poor shot, with a driver will go farther off line than any other club.

If you're having trouble keeping your drives on the fairway, chances are you're suffering from head movement. Strive to make a more controlled swing while keeping your head stock steady, as if in a vise. You'll start making solid contact again, and the extra distance *that* adds will amaze and delight you, and, of course, improve your overall game.

7 Practice

I said in the introduction to this book that if you made an effort to get a grasp of the game's basic principles and devoted the time toward practicing them, you would be rewarded by knocking a substantial amount of strokes off your average score.

I have no doubt about that.

I also have no doubt that more than a few of you rolled your eyes and sighed upon reading that magic word—practice. I've a good idea why. I've heard many complaints from amateurs who claim that none of the time they've spent hitting practice balls has done them any good.

Frankly, I'm sure it doesn't, since they probably don't put in much of what I call *quality* practice time. Usually, they go to the local range, buy a bucket of balls, borrow a driver, seek out the nearest rubber mat, and blast away. Showering the range for half an hour may give your muscles a workout, but it does nothing for your swing.

It's my goal in this chapter to teach you ways to get more out of your practice time, as well as making it more enjoyable. Once you discover what quality practice does for your scoring, it automatically and naturally will become a lot more fun.

THE POINT OF PRACTICE

The goal in golf is not to build a picture-perfect swing but to build a functional swing, and more importantly, a repeatable swing. If you can't swing at the ball the same way twice, you aren't going to have much luck at this game.

That's why practicing is so important. It conditions the muscles and the body to make the proper swing moves until they become automatic and reflexive, or grooved. At that point, you can perform them without any thought when you're on the course.

The course is no place to be worrying about swing mechanics. You should be devoting your full attention to your playing strategy there. Instead, make the practice tee the workshop where you build a sound swing or adjust one that needs fixing. The practice tee can be a very relaxing place. There's no pressure to score or hit each and every shot well. You can experiment without worry. Above all, you have the freedom to take your time between shots and really concentrate on ingraining the proper fundamentals into each and every swing.

Devote each practice session to one or two specific goals. If, for instance, your head position is suspect, make it the goal of that particular session. Forget other mechanical problems; solely work on keeping your head still. Players get discouraged because they tackle too much at once and end up by not getting much of a handle on anything.

FIND A GOOD PLACE

It's important to find a place where the turf resembles real playing conditions. Rubber mats do not fill the bill.

If your course has a practice range, by all means use it. If not, look around and find a place to hit your own shag balls—a local high school, a college athletic field, or similar open space where you can safely make full swings.

ALWAYS HIT TO A TARGET

When you think about it, the most important part of a golf shot is that it goes where you want it to go. Every shot you play during a round of golf is aimed at some kind of target, whether it's an area of the fairway, a part of the green, or the pin itself. It's therefore especially important always to have a target in mind when hitting practice balls.

Don't get into the habit of just swinging away and trying to make good contact. It isn't especially hard to step up to the ball and give it a solid smack, but it is difficult to give the ball a solid smack and have it go exactly where you want it to. I know that it's easier to just hit away without aiming at anything since it gives you one less thing to worry about. However, the next time you're playing on the course you may have plenty to worry about when you find you're hitting everything to the left or right of your target.

Using pointer clubs to develop good aim.

One excellent aid that works wonders for developing and maintaining good aim and alignment is the use of pointer clubs.

First, drop a ball to hit. Lay a club down just outside of it, pointing toward your target. Next, lay down a second club parallel to the first and just outside of where your toes would be at address. You can now set up to the ball knowing that you're aiming at a target, as well as having a reference point for determining the alignment of your feet, hips, and shoulders with each club.

You might even want to lay a third club perpendicular to the others along the line of your left heel, with the butt end of the grip just below the ball, to make sure that the ball position is correct.

Some players use just one club positioned near their feet. I prefer having the second one outside the ball as well for three reasons.

First, it helps clarify the image of being square to, and aiming directly at, your target. It's as if you're standing on railroad tracks that lead straight to where you want the ball to go.

Second, if you make sure that the clubface is set perpendicular to the outside clubshaft, you'll know that it's square to your target line.

Third, having the club just outside the ball helps indicate when your downswing path is bad, since both an overly outside-in path or inside-out path will result in contact between the clubhead and the shaft on the ground.

One of the most common faults that can creep into any player's game, whether he's a high handicapper or a scratch player, is slipping into a poor alignment position at address without realizing it. It can happen very easily *unless* you check yourself periodically. If not, it leads to all sorts of problems, from pulling and hooking to pushing and slicing.

You'll often see Tour pros using pointer clubs on the practice tee. If it works well enough for them, it will work well enough for you.

SPACE YOUR SESSIONS OUT

I'd strongly recommend spacing out your practice sessions throughout the week, rather than putting in one or two long ones. You'll usually get too fatigued by trying to practice for too long, which often leads to picking up bad and lazy habits.

You probably will tire very quickly at the beginning. But resist the temptation to push yourself too hard. Your endurance will build with each session until you'll be able to hit a good many balls without losing your zip.

This is a big help to those players who often run out of gas during the closing holes of a round. You'll have more energy coming down the stretch thanks to the stamina built by your practice.

MAKE PRACTICE FUN

The most important thing you can bring with you to the practice tee is the right attitude. Make practice fun, not drudgery. If you look at it as boring time spent hacking away at balls, then that's what it will be. If you approach it with the attitude that it will help you improve your playing ability and lead to lower scores, you'll find practice much more productive.

I have always loved to practice, because I enjoy hitting the ball, whether it's on the course or on the range. I know that I'm only strengthening my game by being out there practicing.

I'll often pretend I'm playing an entire round from tee to green on one of my favorite courses, hitting every drive and approach shot from the first hole to the eighteenth. My point is that, with the help of the right attitude and your imagination, your practice sessions can be more fun and as a result, more productive.

So stop wasting time. Go out to your workshop and get to work. You can then look forward—realistically—to a better swing and lower scores!

8
Visualization

You probably have heard that playing good golf is mostly mental, and it is. Clear thinking leads to good decisions on strategy. That's a key element in scoring well.

Another equally important mental aspect of the game is *visualization,* the process of imagining what the shot you're about to play will feel and look like before you play it.

This valuable asset will serve you well anywhere on the course, from the tee to the scoring zone to trouble play.

Before you hit any shot, imagine everything about it. The feel of the club in your hands as you grip it; the backswing and the downswing, impact. Then imagine the ball flying to your target and finishing exactly as planned.

Visualizing the shot from start to finish helps activate your muscle memory for playing the shot you want to play. It's especially helpful in a pressure situation. Visualizing the result you want also blocks out negative thoughts.

Even if this is the first time you've formally heard about visualizing a golf shot before hitting it, you probably have done it without realizing it. Think about one of your favorite par-three holes—one where you always feel you'll hit the green. Every time you step up to the tee, memories of past good shots come flooding back. You "see" the ball arching toward the green and automatically "feel" that good 7-iron swing. You gain such confidence from thinking about it that you can't wait to do it again.

That's what good visualization can trigger on *every* shot.

PRACTICING VISUALIZATION

The more you practice visualization, the better you'll get at it, and the more it will help your play.

If you're like me, when you aren't playing golf, you like to relax by thinking about your game. The next time you do, try playing a few holes in your imagination.

Picture yourself on the tee of your favorite par four on a beautiful windless morning. You tee up the ball and survey the situation, picking out a landing area. Take your grip and step up to the ball, relaxed and ready. Make a good swing—*crack*—and it flies straight toward your target.

Now for your second shot. It's on a good lie and 150 yards to the pin, which is tucked behind a bunker guarding the right front of the green. The air is calm, so you take your 5-iron and aim for the middle of the green, playing your normal fade. Take your grip, address, swing—*contact*—and the ball flies first toward the center of the green, then drifts right before settling softly pin high, about ten feet left of the flag.

Finally, your birdie putt. It looks as if it will break a little right to left, so you'll play it about a ball-width outside the right edge. It's slightly uphill, and the grain is against you, so be a little firmer with it. Take your stance, get comfortable, be confident, and stroke. Feels good. Nice roll. Bingo!

Try it the next time your mind drifts off toward golf. It's good mental practice, it's fun, and you'll find you rarely get into trouble or make bogey. Talk about improving your game!

9

The Scoring Zone

The scoring zone is that area of every hole from approximately fifty yards to the green. It's where the short game is played. Players who are proficient in this area of their games save themselves a ton of strokes, while those who aren't often waste many.

The short game has long been referred to as the great equalizer, and it truly is, because a shorter hitting player can more than make up for his lack of distance by having a deft touch around the green. There's little doubt that chipping and pitching the ball close and one-putting have scored countless birdies and saved many a par for me and other Tour pros. None of us underestimate the value of the shots needed in the scoring zone: the chip and the pitch shots.

You can get a better idea of the importance of playing these shots well by estimating the average number of greens you hit in regulation per round. Let's say the number is nine. If you can get the ball "up and down" each time that's *nine* strokes saved!

THE CHIP

The chip shot is played from just off the green, about a yard or two from the edge to ten yards away. It is easiest to view it as an extension of putting. Because of this, I've found it most comfortable to chip with the same type of stroke I use on the green. I'd advise you to do the same, whether your natural motion is wristy, stiff-wristed, or a combination of the two. You may even use your putting grip if it feels comfortable and helps you with your stroke.

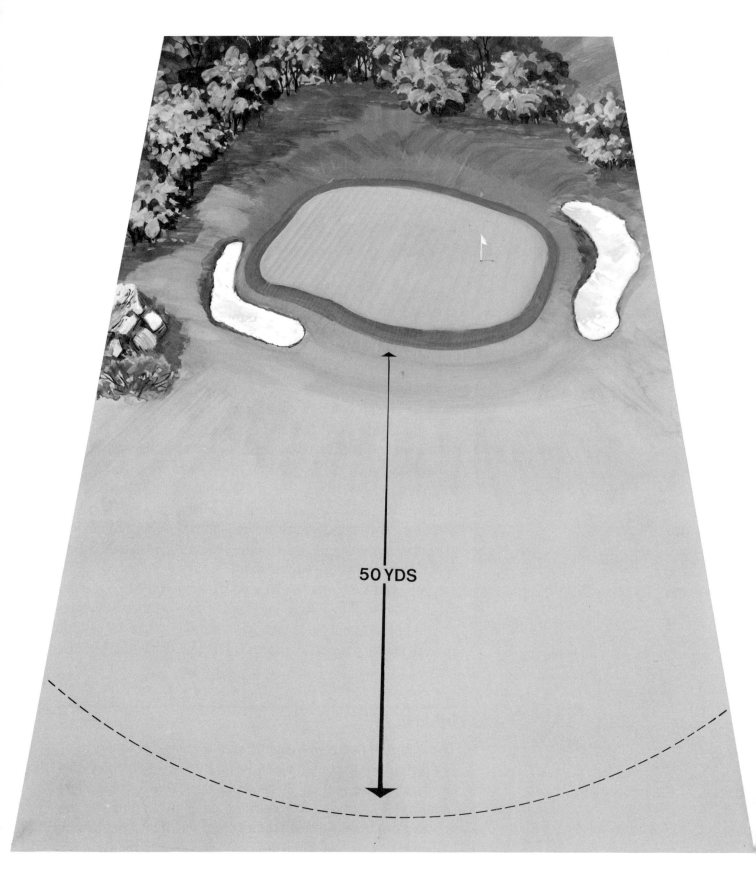

The scoring zone: from fifty yards in.

There is, however, a standard address position that must be learned. It will help you make consistently crisp, solid contact every time. Set up to the ball in a very narrow, open stance. Put most of your weight on your left side. Choke down on the club for control and play the ball well back off your right toe, with your hands set well ahead of it. You should feel as though you're in a very compact, very solid position at address, but still relaxed. On the downstroke, be sure to keep your hands well ahead and hit the ball first, to prevent scooping, or chili-dipping, it.

Although the chip is the most delicate shot you'll have to play in golf next to a short putt, you still have to be sure to *accelerate* into the ball. There are few things more frustrating than making a weak downswing and stubbing a chip, because it really is a fairly simple shot to play given the right technique.

Keeping your head still when both chipping and pitching is just as important as on full-swing shots. Guard against letting it waver, or move.

The key to chipping consistently close is to get the ball down on the surface and rolling like a putt as soon as possible. I always visualize landing the ball on the green about two feet in from the fringe and letting it run from there. Always aim to land the ball on the putting surface, rather than risk a bad bounce or have the ball slowed down by the froghair.

I'd recommend using various clubs for chipping, basing your selection on the distance of the ball from the edge of the green. From a couple of yards off I'll use a 4-iron and go up a club for every couple of yards farther away. By varying the clubs used in this way, you'll find you won't have to worry as much about varying the force of your stroke.

Try using a variety of clubs to chip with. It's a lot easier than if you restrict yourself to using just one.

One final note, use the putter as often as you can when just off the green. It doesn't make sense to me when I see a player who is a foot or two off the putting surface using any other club than the putter. Why? Because nine times out of ten, you'll get the ball as close to the hole with your worst putt as you would with your best chip.

If you're no more than a few feet off in the fringe, go with the putter and treat the shot as just another long putt. By taking the variable of airtime out of the chip and keeping it on the ground, you'll end up putting the ball closer to the hole a lot more often than you would using any other club.

For a chip shot, set up in a very narrow, open stance. Play the ball off the right toe and set the hands well ahead of it.

My backswing is wristy—similar to my putting stroke. You'll do best to chip with the same type of stroke you use to putt with.

It's crucial to accelerate downward into the ball to avoid mishitting the shot.

Keeping the head still on a chip is as important as on a full shot, so don't let it lift until well after contact has been made.

Using two targets, pick out an area on the green as the first target and concentrate on landing the ball on that spot, making the hole the second target.

THE SHORT PITCH

As you get farther from the green, say ten yards, or more, you'll be beyond the range where the chipping stroke will do you any good—you're in pitching territory.

Although the chipping stroke was closely related to the putting stroke, the pitching stroke has more arms in it and more closely resembles the full swing.

To play a short pitch, take an open, narrow stance, the same width as for chipping, with most of your weight on your left side. Take your pitching wedge and choke down for control, opening the clubface slightly. Keep your backswing short and crisp and accelerate firmly down into the ball staying dead-wristed through impact. Consciously prevent the right hand from rolling over the left so that you keep the blade open through the ball. This is basically an arms only swing, so make a strong effort to keep your body motion, especially the lower body, very still.

To hit the ball close to the pin on short pitches, you must plan and visualize the shot from start to finish.

Try to think of the shot as having two targets to best estimate the necessary amount of carry and roll. I make the

A CRUCIAL CHIP

I captured the 1962 Masters Tournament at Augusta National Golf Club in Augusta, Georgia, by winning an eighteen-hole playoff over Gary Player and Dow Finsterwald. The most important shot of that tournament and one of the most important of my career came on the par-three sixteenth hole in the final round.

Standing on the tee, I knew I was two shots behind Player and Finsterwald, who was already in the clubhouse with a 280. The pin on the sixteenth was cut in the back left corner of the green, but I pushed my 3-iron shot slightly, putting it on the fringe about ten feet from the edge of the surface.

From there I faced a slick, downhill chip. I had to land the ball on the right spot at the right speed to get it close. I layed a wedge that landed right on target and rolled into the cup for a birdie two. I followed that with another birdie on the par-four seventeenth hole to finish in a three-way tie with Player and Finsterwald, which I won on the following day for my third Masters victory.

For a short pitch, set up in a very open,
narrow stance, choke down on the club
and open the face.

The swing is made mainly with the arms,
with body motion kept to a minimum.

Accelerate firmly down through the ball with a dead-wristed action, keeping the blade from closing through impact.

The clubface should be facing the sky in the follow-through.

spot where I'd like to land the ball my first target and the pin my second target. As a general rule, figure on negotiating about two-thirds of the distance in carry and the remaining one-third in roll.

With that in mind, determine the spot on the green where you want to land the ball and concentrate on carrying the shot to that target. Forget about the pin. If you hit your spot, chances are you'll end up close to the hole.

THE LONG PITCH

On a longer pitch, your main objective should be to hit a very high, soft-landing shot that will stop quickly next to the flag. To best accomplish this, set up in a narrow, open stance, slightly wider than for the short pitch, with your weight mostly to the left.

The key to getting a high, arching trajectory is to keep your hands and wrists firm through impact. It should feel as though you're sliding the clubface underneath the ball and through the grass without taking much of a divot.

THE PITCH OF MY LIFE

The shot that most people remember about my victory in the 1961 British Open at Royal Birkdale in England is the 6-iron I played from the rough at the fifteenth hole in the final round (see page 161.) But I can remember another critical shot—one that occurred in the third round—a pitch that turned what had appeared to be a certain seven or eight into a par.

On the sixteenth hole, a par four of 404 yards, I hit my second shot too strongly, and it was only stopped by a bush behind the green. As I walked to the green, I mentally prepared myself for an unplayable lie. At first glance, the only option appeared to be dropping away from the bush for a penalty stroke. I couldn't see a clear route through the foliage to the flagstick. Then, as I was about to give up, I noticed a small gap in the branches, just large enough for a golf ball to pass through.

I took my sand wedge, laid the blade wide open so it almost faced the sky, then hit down hard. The ball jumped almost straight up into the air, spun and finished inches from the hole. My playing partner, Kel Nagle, was kind enough to join in the applause of the crowd.

I'm still proud of that one.

It's important to keep your body motion to a minimum—this, too, is mainly an arms swing.

Probably the most difficult thing about playing long pitches is learning to vary the yardages you hit them. It comes down to the difference in feel between pitching a ball, say thirty yards and pitching it forty.

A good way to develop this feel for distance on long pitches is to practice what I call the ten-yard drill. I'll hit five balls to a target starting from twenty yards away, then five from thirty yards, five from forty yards, and so on, until I'm about a full wedge away. Then I'll start moving in until I'm back where I started.

By running through this drill from time to time, you will work wonders in getting your long pitches closer.

SHORT GAME PRACTICE

Professional players devote a great deal of their practice time to shots played in the scoring zone. Even though they're fine strikers of the ball, they don't hit every green in regulation, and a solid short game is the only defense against making more than par when they do miss a green.

Adopt the same attitude and allot a good percentage of your practice time to learning and getting a feel for the shots required around the green.

You'll find a good short game is the best backup you can have for saving par when your long game goes awry, and, when you're playing well, can really help you score in the low numbers.

10 Putting

Putting is the one part of the game with the fewest existing guidelines. There is no one right way to wield the putter. This is clearly demonstrated by the many great players who have earned the reputations of being excellent putters while employing widely varying styles and strategies. You are free and I encourage you to develop an individual style that works best for you.

In my years on Tour, I've seen many different types of strokes among good putters. Some use a great deal of wrist action, others more of an arm-and-shoulders stroke. Some set up with a very upright posture, while others hunker down low over the ball. No one can say which method is right and which is wrong because there *is* no right or wrong. No one can teach another person the *right* way to putt because none exists.

What I can do, however, is pass on to you some of the fundamentals that are common to the strokes of all the good putters. Though your stroke should be based on personal comfort and preference, these are things that you must incorporate into your putting style.

THE COMMON DENOMINATORS OF GOOD PUTTING

The first fundamental is our old friend, the still head. On full swings, keeping your head still helps ensure returning the clubface squarely to the ball. Your head plays the same role during the putting stroke.

Making solid contact is crucial to establishing good roll on your putts. If you've been coming up short on many of your putts, check your head movement; it's the prime cause of mishit putts. Be especially sure to stay set during and through impact. Try to see the putter strike the back of the ball before looking up.

Another fundamental common to all good putters is their balance. Whether their stances are wide or narrow, open or closed, whether their postures are upright or hunched over, all good putters I've ever seen distributed their weight equally between their feet to form a comfortable and solid foundation.

I prefer to bend fairly low at the waist and set up with a somewhat narrow, square stance. How you do it is up to you. Just make sure you're in balance. If your body is unstable and moving around during the stroke, the chances of consistently sending the ball along the chosen line will be almost nil.

The last fundamental is the putter's ability to keep *both hands* moving toward the target through impact, while maintaining a firm left wrist. Whether the left wrist is cupped or square with the left forearm at address is up to you, but you must not allow it to collapse through impact. Strive for the feeling of *pulling* the clubhead through the ball, with both hands working as one unit. That way you'll keep the blade moving forward along the intended line.

PUTTING GRIPS

One element of putting that varies widely from player to player is the grip. Many golfers take a different style grip on the putter than for full shots because it gives them a better sense of feel or helps them execute the type of stroke they prefer.

The ten-finger grip, as its name suggests, puts all your fingers on the grip, providing better feedback and touch.

The reverse overlap grip, which some people credit me with popularizing, places the index finger of the left hand either over the little finger of the right hand or across all the fingers of the right hand. It helps deaden your wrist action and keeps your left wrist firm throughout the stroke. It probably is the most commonly used putting grip today.

The great putters, however, have used all sorts of grips. The late Bobby Locke used the standard overlapping grip. He didn't see any point in changing the grip for putting. Byron Nelson combines the overlap and reverse overlap grips. He overlaps the third finger of his left hand with the little finger of his right hand while reverse-overlapping the first three fingers

Because balance is crucial to good putting, be sure to take a wide enough stance to establish a solid foundation.

The still head has the same function in the putting stroke as it does in the full-swing: It helps ensure returning the putterface to the ball squarely.

Keep both hands moving toward the target through impact while maintaining a firm left wrist.

Keep the head down and body still until well after impact.

From this angle, you can see how close I keep my hands to my body during the stroke. Whether you prefer them positioned close or farther away depends upon what feels most comfortable.

On the forward swing, I strive to pull my hands through the ball with the feeling that both are working as a single unit.

Continue moving the blade along the intended line in the follow-through.

Never look up until well after the ball has been struck.

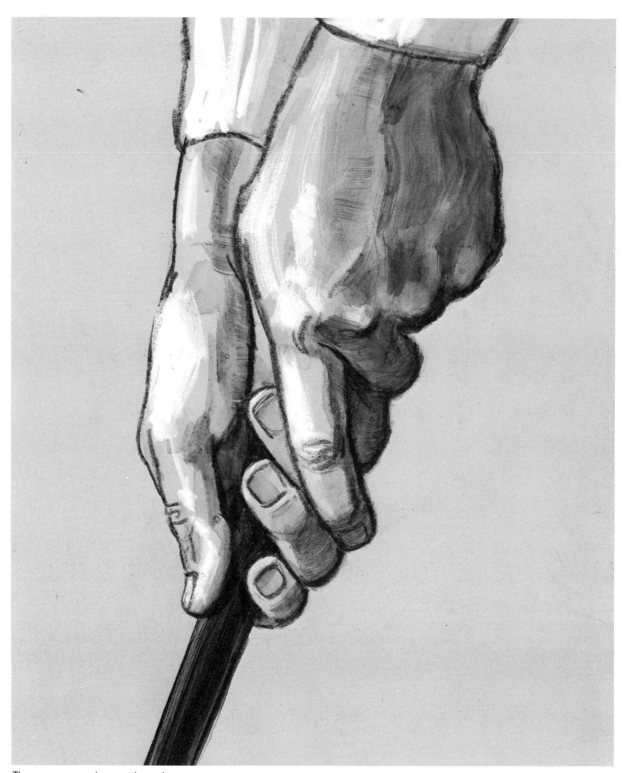

The reverse overlap putting grip.

of his right hand with the left index finger. He then digs the fingernail of his right thumb into the grip.

On the Tour today are some fine players who don't use the reverse overlap. Hubert Green has been very successful with the split-handed grip, his right hand separate from, and very much below, his left. Bruce Lietzke uses the cross-handed grip, left hand below right. Bernhard Langer uses the reverse overlap on long putts, then switches to the cross-handed grip on short putts.

Whatever grip you choose, don't be afraid to experiment with it. Try moving a finger here or there until you're comfortable. You might even end up inventing your own putting grip. Although everyone should learn a textbook grip for full-swing shots, how you hold the putter should be dictated by what feels and works best for you.

PUTTING STRATEGY

Putting strategy is similar to a full-scale playing strategy. It's the game plan you set up on the green to get the ball into the cup with the fewest number of strokes. Just as you'll almost never face the same exact shot twice from tee to green, rarely will you face a putt that is exactly like another in break, length, and speed. These variables are the reasons why being a good putter takes a great deal of thought and concentration besides having a good stroke.

I'd like to pass on some of my thoughts on putting strategy to help you eliminate some of those three-putt greens while increasing the number of times you one-putt.

LONG PUTTS

Think about the variables just mentioned—length, speed, and break. There's a lot going on there, and the longer the putt, the more these variables come into play. On very undulating greens, you may have a putt that will take as many as three breaks before reaching the hole. Your primary goal on long putts should be getting down in two instead of trying to sink the ball on the first try. Even the pros, who sink their share of long ones, almost always have two-putting as their goal when they step up to one of thirty feet or longer.

I always feel just a little bit lucky when I make a long one because, hey, let's not kid ourselves, that cup is a pretty small

6 FEET

To avoid three-putting, aim for a six-foot circle around the cup.

target, especially from fifty feet away. It amuses me when I see players agonizing time after time over failing to drop putts of this length. If you happen to be leaving long second putts—averaging more than three feet, then you *do* have reason to agonize. But if you're consistently leaving the ball within three feet of the cup, then ease up on yourself and consider it a job well done.

If you are having three-putt problems because you're not getting the ball close enough to the cup on your first attempt, try enlarging the target by creating an imaginary circle six feet in diameter around the cup. Getting the ball inside this circle will leave you with a very makeable second putt. Devote most of your concentration toward rolling the ball the proper distance. Break won't be as important as before, because now you have a hole six feet wide. The hardest part of this task is to hit the ball at the proper speed in order to lag the ball into the circle. Of course, the better you get at finishing the long ones within the big circle, the more often they will drop!

BILLY CASPER'S BEST BIRDIE

In the final round of the U.S. Open at Olympic Club in San Francisco in 1966, I was seven shots ahead of Billy Casper with nine holes to play. As we came to the fifteenth hole, my lead had shrunk to five, yet that seemed plenty to get me safely home. I still had a good chance of coming in with a 275 to beat Ben Hogan's Open record of 276.

The fifteenth is a par three, 147 yards long. The green is slightly elevated and surrounded by bunkers. The pin was tightly tucked on the right side, so Billy played a safe 7-iron to the fat of the green on the left. Preoccupied with beating Hogan's record, I went for the "perfect" shot—right at the cup. Had the ball hit an inch to the left of where it did, it would have kicked left and stopped near the hole for a good birdie chance, but it didn't. Instead, the ball trickled down into the right-hand bunker. I hit a good explosion to eight feet of the pin. Then Billy stuck it to me. From twenty feet away, he aimed well left to allow for the break and holed the putt for a birdie. I missed my putt and, for the first time, I realized that Casper could catch me.

He did just that, tying me at 278, then winning the playoff, 69 to 73.

DYING VERSUS CHARGING

There are two basic ways of rolling a putt to the hole once you get into the range where sinking the putt becomes your goal and the actual cup becomes your target.

The first is known as *dying* the ball to the cup, or hitting it with just enough speed so it reaches its destination and drops in. You must hit the ball at near-perfect speed and play the break perfectly.

One advantage of this method is that you can use the whole cup. That means the ball usually has only to catch an edge of the cup to topple in. Its chances of lipping out are low because of its slow rate of speed.

The second advantage is that if you miss, you'll almost always have a very short second putt.

The second way to go about getting the ball to the hole is known as *charging* the cup, and involves making the back of the cup your target and firmly stroking the ball for it. Charging the cup has long been my favorite method, and I guess it's one of the most famous parts of my game. As one who has favored playing aggressively from tee to green, this aggressive putting style comes naturally to me.

The main advantage in charging the cup is that it allows a player to focus on a specific target, namely the back of the cup, and to make an aggressive stroke for it. You don't have to worry about hitting it at perfect speed or having read the break perfectly. Almost every time you'll get the ball to the hole.

The disadvantage to charging is that, if you don't roll the ball squarely into the back side of the cup, your chances of lipping out are a lot greater. You'll also, on the average, face longer second putts if you miss than if you die the ball to the hole.

It's funny that part of my reputation as a good putter came because I made a lot of putts in the six- to eight-foot range during my career. I faced a lot of putts of that length because I had charged the ball past the cup that far on my first putts.

You don't have to hit the ball that hard to be a good charge putter. What I do is to plan on leaving myself no more than a three-foot putt coming back if I miss.

Your choice of putting style probably reflects the style you normally play with from tee to green. Players who naturally play aggressively generally choose a charging style; those who always play the percentages usually favor dying the ball to the cup.

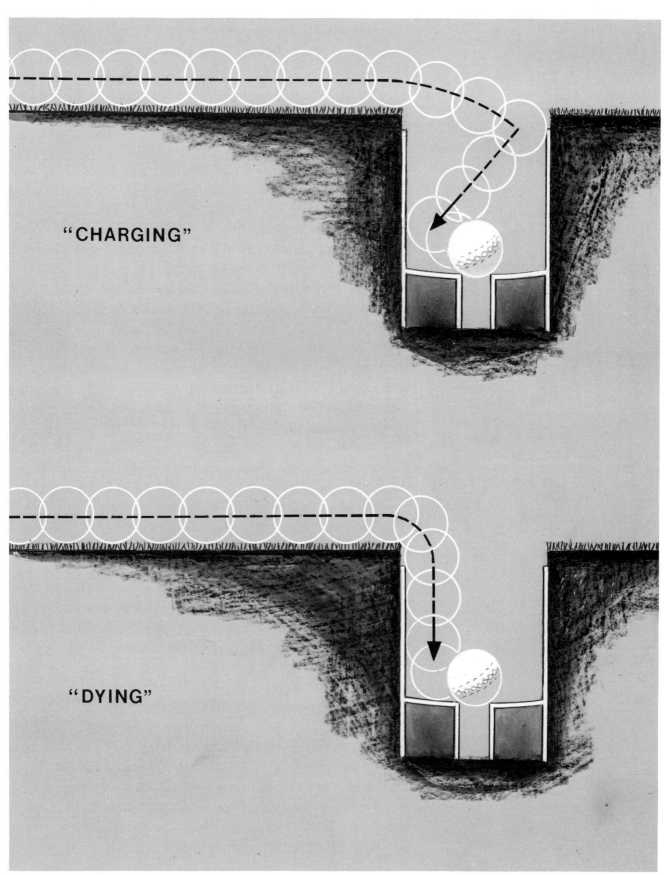

"CHARGING"

"DYING"

The two ways to sink a putt.

Remember, the bottom line is to get the ball to the bottom of the cup in as few strokes as possible. Whichever style works best for you is the one you should stick with.

SHORT PUTTS

If the ball lies within about five feet of the hole, it's a *short* putt.

I've always believed that whether you choose to charge the cup or die the ball to it on your makeable putts, the way you'll hole most of the short putts is to stroke them firmly to the back of the cup. Your odds of hitting your mark are very good due to the shortness of the putt. If you should happen to miss, you still won't run too far past.

This method is especially good for sidehill putts. It allows you to worry less about the break and lets you focus more on the cup.

Short uphill putts present an even better chance for you to be firm with your stroke, since the angle of the slope makes the back of the cup higher in relation to the front, giving you a backstop. Always try to take full advantage of this situation by giving the ball a good, firm rap.

I take exception to this rule, however, when facing a slippery downhiller. Then I try to ease the ball into the cup rather than run the risk of letting it get away down the hill if I miss. Besides that, when the slope is away from you, the back of the cup is slightly lower than the front, so a firm putt has a good chance of running right over the hole.

A good technique to use on slick downhill putts is to address the ball slightly toward the toe of the blade and away from the sweet spot. This method deadens the impact and prevents the ball from jumping too quickly down the slope.

The sweet spot is the area of the clubface that will produce the most solid impact possible. It is not always in the exact middle of the blade, however.

To find the sweet spot on your putter, hold it by the butt end of the grip between the thumb and forefinger of your left hand, letting it hang straight down with the clubface facing you. Tap the face lightly with the knuckle of your right index finger. The blade may twist and turn a little—if it does, keep tapping until you find the spot that sends the putterhead straight backward. *That's* the sweet spot, the part of the face you should try to stroke all your putts with.

A FIVE-FOOT SIDEHILLER

On the seventy-second green of the 1960 Masters, a five-foot sidehill putt stood between me and outright victory. Watching in the clubhouse was Ken Venturi, anticipating an eighteen-hole playoff the next day if I missed.

I had started the final round a stroke ahead of Venturi and two strokes up on Dow Finsterwald, but I had let my lead slip away and fallen one stroke behind Venturi by the time I reached the par-four seventeenth tee, who had finished at five under. But a thirty-five foot birdie there drew me into a tie for the lead.

But on the eighteenth tee, a tie was the furthest thing from my mind. I hit a solid drive into the wind down the middle and followed it with 6-iron punched under the breeze that stopped five feet from the pin.

At that point in my career, it probably was the most important putt I'd ever faced, and I was plenty nervous. I read it to break about three or four inches from left to right, stroked it smoothly and watched it catch the left side and drop in for my second Masters victory.

It's a good idea to check for the location of the sweet spot even if the manufacturer has already indicated one with a mark on top. Sometimes those marks are off. If yours is, or if it doesn't have an indicator at all, you may want to put a piece of tape above where the sweet spot is to remind yourself where you want to strike the ball.

THE PSYCHOLOGY OF SHORT PUTTS

A short putt can be one of the most psychologically demanding parts of the game. Because of its length, every golfer, pros and amateurs alike, feels compelled to make it; feels he's *expected* to make it. When he doesn't hole it, he thinks he's missed an easy shot. He ruminates, "It took you one swing of the driver to put the ball 250 yards down the fairway, while it's taken you *two* strokes with the putter to get it into the cup from three feet away! How *could* you have missed?"

Of course it's not all right to miss a short putt, because it will cost a stroke when you do, but don't expect to make them all.

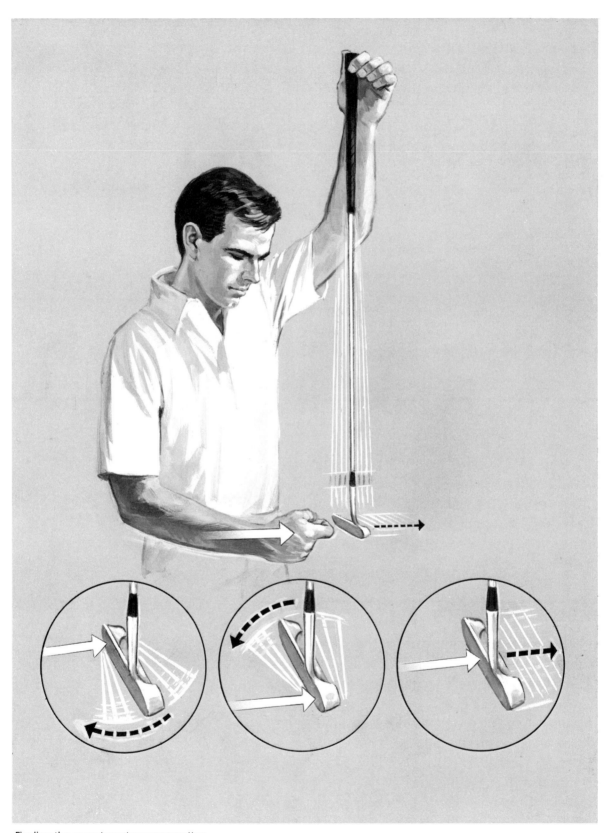

Finding the sweet spot on your putter.

Take it easy on yourself when you do miss one. It's bound to happen sometimes. But don't compound the mistake by letting it eat away at your overall confidence.

On the one hand, nothing builds your confidence better than sinking the first two four-footers you face during your Saturday morning round. You step up to the next green armed with the memory of the last two plunking into the cup, and chances are you drill that putt in too. The confidence tends to snowball.

On the other hand, nothing destroys your confidence more than missing the first couple of short putts. You sidle up to the next one with the vision of your last failures looming large in your head, not even able to concentrate on executing a good stroke. You end up missing mainly because you were afraid of missing.

Sometimes you can lose so much confidence you become a victim of the yips. You become so scared of missing any short putt that you physically can't make a good stroke.

The best advice I can give you when your confidence is really shot is to hit the practice green and find it again. Try something new—a grip variation or a slight change in address, something to give you a new feeling and confidence over the ball.

Work at making your confidence snowball in the other direction. Tell yourself you aren't going to leave the green until you sink 15 three-footers in a row; then 10 four-footers in a row; and 5 five-footers. If you can successfully complete this drill a few times, you'll have a whole new outlook the next time you're standing over a short putt on the course. Trust me.

GREEN READING

It would certainly simplify the act of putting if every green were flat, making every putt roll dead straight. The fact is, it's very rare indeed when we do face a putt with no break at all and one that is neither uphill nor downhill.

Instead, a putt's line will nearly always be affected to some degree by the slopes and undulations of the ground. This effect is greater on a putt than on any other shot in golf, since it travels every inch of the way from clubface to the hole along the ground.

There are a number of variables that must be taken into account that may have an effect on the speed and line of the putt. The better you are at determining how the putt will react to these variables, the better your chances are of sinking it. You could have the finest putting stroke in the world, but if you can't figure out how a particular putt will break and approximately what speed to hit it, you won't make very many.

Break

The first thing I like to determine is the direction the putt will break due to the slope of the surface between my ball and the cup. If it slopes from left to right, the putt will break from left to right; if it slopes from right to left, the putt will break from right to left.

That's fairly straightforward and simple. The trick, however, is in determining how much the putt will break and sometimes in determining which way the slope goes. It's not always easy to tell this when the green is one with subtle rolls and undulations.

My standard procedure for reading the break is to squat down behind the ball and simply use my eyes to pick up the angle of the slope. I like to get an idea of the general slope of a green as I approach it from the fairway. You'll find, as I do, that a more distant view often will give you a better idea of the slope and topography of a green than when you are up close to it. This knowledge will help a great deal when you're undecided.

Occasionally, you'll face a putt with a double-break. In that case, use the two-target system, making your first target the spot where you think the second break will start, and putt for that. It's tough enough to figure out one break, let alone two, so getting the ball close to the hole is a pretty good effort on double-breaking putts.

Uphill/Downhill

You also have to take into account whether or not the slope of the green is uphill or downhill. This will have a direct effect on the overall speed of your putt.

Very simply, going uphill will make the speed slower, while going downhill will add to it. This may sound obvious, but I've often seen players become so involved in reading the break that they forget to take the slope factor into consideration.

To read the break, I prefer squatting
behind the ball and using my eyes to pick
out the character of the slope.

Remember that putting uphill gives you the advantage of having the back of the cup slightly higher than the front, so go firmly for the back. On downhillers, a ball can easily roll right over the middle of the cup, so have it approach the hole gently.

Grain

Another variable in putting that has a direct, though subtle, effect on both the speed and break of a putt is the *grain* of the green. Grain is the direction in which the blades of grass grow. It's a part of the putting game that I think far too few amateurs ever consider.

If the grain is running in the same direction as the break, the ball will tend to break more than expected. If the grain runs against it, the ball will break less. If the grain runs toward the hole, the speed of a putt will be faster; while grain against you slows your ball down.

Determining the direction of the grain on a green isn't always easy, since the blades of grass grow so densely, but there are several ways to read it.

Look at the surface of the green. If it has a sheen to it, the grain is running away from you. A dull surface means the grain is running toward you.

Grain also tends to grow in the direction of water. Keep an eye out for any nearby ponds or similar bodies of water that might help you determine grain direction.

Note the contours of a green, since grain usually grows down slopes, in the same direction that water would drain.

If the direction of the grain still has you puzzled, here is one last tip. Take a look at the edge of the cup, where the blades of grass should be hanging slightly over one side, showing the direction in which they're growing.

Get the Read and Go

Once you've determined how a putt will react to a particular set of variables on a given green, trust your decision and then concentrate on making a good stroke. Indecision almost always leads to deceleration, even in putting, and invariably results in a poor effort.

I know that I'd rather miss with a confident stroke than make a weak attempt that never had a chance.

Indecision inevitably erodes confidence. Have faith in the "read" and go for it.

PUTTING VISUALIZATION

It's just as important to visualize your putts as it is any other golf shot. Imagine the feel of the putter in your hands, the rhythm of the stroke, the sound of impact; watch in your mind's eye as the ball rolls along the line, takes the break, and drops in the cup. I like to think of the ball as sitting on a pair of railroad tracks that run straight into the hole. When I stroke the ball, it will ride over them straight into the bottom of the cup.

If you're having a tough time picturing the line of your putts, try getting out to the practice green when the dew is still on the grass. Your putts will leave distinct paths as they roll, giving you precise images you can use in the future.

The importance of using mental imagery in putting cannot be stressed enough. You can try my idea of the ball on a pair of railroad tracks. You can imagine all your putts rolling along a dew-covered green. You can even invent something different, such as coloring the path to the hole with a hue that appeals to you—gold, red, whatever you like. It really doesn't matter what mental image you conjure up; just find one that works for you and *use it*.

Visualize each and every one of your putts, both long and short. *See* the long ones roll lazily into the imaginary circle around the hole. *Watch* the short ones bang into the back of the cup and hear them rattle to the bottom.

You'll gain a lot of confidence if you make visualization a regular part of your putting routine. If there's a secret to great putting, visualization is it.

PUTTING: ANYONE CAN BE GOOD AT IT

It doesn't take great strength or physical ability to be a good putter. Not everyone is able to drive a golf ball 260 yards, but anyone from the tallest to the smallest can develop a fine putting game if they work at it. I've seen some golfers who could barely drive a ball 150 yards off the tee who are great putters, because they've taken the time to work at it.

I've also seen golfers who hit the ball well from tee-to-green who were less than adequate with the putter, which

To visualize a putt, you can imagine the ball riding railroad tracks into the hole.

frustrates them greatly. Most players who suffer from this imbalance in their games do so because they devote too much practice time to their long game and not enough to their short game.

When you think about it, you're allotted thirty-six strokes for every eighteen holes you play, just for putting. That's *one-half* the strokes allowed on a par-72 course! This simple mathematics alone should convince you how important putting is to good scoring.

The next time you play, count the number of strokes you take. If it's more than thirty-six, your putting needs work. It also may indicate that the rest of your short game needs practice. The reason you're taking so many putts may be that you aren't getting the ball into one-putt range from the scoring zone.

Being a good putter can help you make up for what you lack in other parts of the game, making average ball-strikers good scorers; and good ball-strikers excellent scorers. You may hit an errant drive here or a poor approach shot there, but you can always make up for it with one or two good putts.

PART III

STRATEGY

Playing great golf is more than just ball-striking—it's scoring. How well you score greatly depends on how well you put all of your individual skills and abilities to work at once and attack a course. Every player, regardless of skill level, should always have a clear-cut strategy, or plan, in mind on how they would like to play a particular hole. It's really another type of visualization. If you have a clear plan in mind, you'll often be successful, or at least come close. But to fire away without a plan means the ball can finish literally anywhere.

Strategy can be broken down into three basic categories.

The first I call *Go for Broke* because it's a very aggressive style of play, where you take a lot of risks for the sake of scoring.

The second type of strategy is just the opposite. I call it *Bailing Out,* because it avoids potential trouble at all costs, sometimes to the point of hitting away from the green.

The third strategy I've labeled *Playing Safe.* It's basically a combination of the first two. A fair amount of risk is involved in playing the course but so is a fair amount of caution.

11
The Thinking Game

MATCHING YOUR STRATEGY TO YOUR SKILLS

The most important factor in choosing a playing strategy is to pick one that fits both your golfing ability and your playing personality.

All of us would agree that an excellent strategy on most par-four holes would be to crack a 280-yard drive down the middle of the fairway, knock the ball close to the pin with a short iron and make birdie. But how many players can realistically expect to do this? "You dance with who you brung," they say in the South, meaning you must *match your strategy to your skills.*

I had an experience once while playing in a pro-am that clearly illustrates my point about planning your strategy around your playing skills.

The player in question knew only one strategy, and that was to hit the ball as far as he could from the tee and shoot for every pin, no matter where he was or what surrounded it. As a second-year player, he had a decent feel for swing mechanics, but in my estimation he had no idea how to think his way around the course.

Throughout the day I watched him haul off with his driver and fire at every flag, no matter what kind of hazards were guarding it. Of course, he got into all kinds of trouble.

"If I could just make a bogey," he moaned as he tapped in for a seven on the fourteenth, a par four.

I didn't say anything to him, but noticed that he had his driver out on the next tee, a par five with a particularly tight driving area. I asked him where he planned to place his drive.

He looked at me, rather perplexed, and answered, "As far out in the fairway as I can hit it."

I then asked him if he thought he could get home in two, and he told me he hadn't really thought about it, but probably couldn't since the hole measured all of 545 yards. Well, I suggested, why not tee off with the 3-wood for control since maximum distance wasn't crucial? Not a bad idea, he agreed.

I went on to ask him about his penchant for flying the ball at the flagstick on every approach shot. "Well," he answered matter of factly, "isn't that what we're all out here for, to score as low as we can?"

I assured him that it was, but added a reminder that his quest for birdies was resulting in a good number of double and triple bogeys. "Don't you think it would be a better idea sometimes to steer away from the pin if the chances are pretty good that you might put it in a trap?" I asked. "You just said you wished you could make bogey. You probably could if you stopped playing for a birdie all the time."

He looked thoughtful for a moment, nodded, and said, "I never really thought of it that way . . . hmmm . . . that really makes me think . . ."

My point exactly. Not enough amateurs really *think*. There's no rule in golf that says you have to hit the driver or even a 3-wood off the tee. *The key to golf is to play the ball to the best position from which to play the next shot.* Where you place the ball off the tee is usually more important than how far you hit it. Shooting for the pin may also seem heroic, but if the percentages are so high against you, what's the point?

RISKS VERSUS GAMBLING

Poor decisions are the greatest cause of most high scores by weekend golfers. Further, they make these bad decisions, I feel, because they really don't understand the difference between taking a *risk* and taking a *gamble*.

A risk is when I know I can play the shot required, say, nine times out of ten, yet there are certain hazards present that may cost me a penalty if I don't pull off the shot as planned. Hitting risky shots are a large part of the game—playing one successfully can provide you with some of your greatest thrills in golf and are often crucial to low scoring.

A shot becomes a gamble when I'm just *hoping* I can play it. If my chances of a successful execution are only one in ten,

I'd be better off playing safe or even bailing out to avoid a disaster.

Despite my reputation as a go-for-broke player, I never have tried a shot in a tournament that I wasn't sure I could make. That's the crucial difference. Too many amateurs take gambles while expecting to make career shots. Once in a while you might make out, but more often than not you simply inflate your score.

Remember, if you truly do not yet have the skills to attack a certain situation, you are the one who will be penalized if you attempt the gamble and lose.

It's fine if you get a thrill out of gambling in difficult situations, but if you're also interested in scoring better, I think you'd better seriously re-examine your strategy. I'm talking to you low handicappers, too. There are plenty of players with great swings who could also knock several strokes off their scores if they used their heads a little better.

CONFIDENCE

There is one key to maximizing your chances of making the shot when a risk is involved, and it's having *confidence* in your ability to play it. If there's doubt in your mind and you aren't sure you can pull the shot off, you'll become apprehensive. You'll start thinking of potential disaster, which results in tension that actually inhibits your physical ability to swing well. Your motion becomes tentative and leads to deceleration.

If you're confident, however, in your ability to perform the task, then your mind will be filled with images of the fine shot you're about to play. This image then will block the hazards present out of your mind and allow you to put a good, accelerating stroke on the ball.

Part of my own preference for the go-for-broke strategy stems from the high degree of confidence that I bring with me to the course. Playing safe just doesn't fit my personality and often makes me decelerate into the ball. I feel more comfortable attacking the course rather than playing it cautiously. Even when I have a substantial lead, I tend to play hard. I have won a lot of tournaments with this strategy. I'll also admit that I occasionally have lost a few when some of the risks I took failed. But I wouldn't have done it any other way.

Players with lower-key personalities than mine may be more confident in themselves playing more cautiously. It's not

GOING FOR BROKE IN THE '60 U.S. OPEN

There have been a lot of times when I used the go for broke strategy in tournament competition, but the time where it paid off most was in the final round of the 1960 U.S. Open at Cherry Hills Country Club.

Starting out seven strokes behind leader Mike Souchak, I knew I couldn't be timid if I wanted any chance at winning. I had to attack the course.

On the par-four first hole, I tried to and successfully drove the green to make birdie (see page 61). I chipped in from thirty-five feet on the second hole for another birdie. On the par-four third my drive was just short of the green and I chipped to a foot away for another birdie, then wedged to within eighteen feet on the fourth and sank the putt for my fourth consecutive birdie. A par on the fifth was followed by a twenty-five foot putt for a deuce on the 174 yard par-three sixth and a six foot putt for a sixth birdie on the par-four seventh hole.

My strategy had worked: six birdies in seven holes and a front nine score of 30 had put me right in the thick of things. But the day wasn't over yet, since the back nine at Cherry Hills is a tough test. I played steadily the rest of the way for a solid two-under par 35 on the back for a score of 65 and the U.S. Open crown.

---

that they lack self-confidence, it's just that they feel more comfortable playing a safer shot instead of pressing every time. They usually play a better game because of it, too.

It's entirely up to you to find out where your confidence lies. Weigh your skills, the particular situation, and your personality and you should come up with the answer.

Let's look at a typical course situation and see how we would apply each of the three types of strategies.

Imagine we're on a par-four hole, (see illustration) about 400 yards long. The tee shot has been well-placed in the middle of the fairway, leaving the ball 150 yards from the pin (most players will choose a 6- or 7-iron for this shot). A pond skirts the front and left side of the green, which is also guarded by a greenside bunker to the right. The ball lies on a part of the fairway that is elevated in relation to the green. The lie is good and the ground is level. The pin is cut close to the left edge of the green, so going for it requires flirting with the water—a one-stroke penalty if you drop it in the drink.

Decision making time . . .

A—Going for broke; B—Playing safe; C—Bailing out.

The skilled player is the best candidate to go for broke here. Should he risk the hazards present to shoot for the pin? He knows he's pretty adept at sand play, so he'll still have a pretty good shot at making par even if he puts the ball in the bunker. The pond to the left and front should be his major consideration. Should he risk putting his shot in the water by going for the pin? After careful consideration, he concludes that he's got the confidence to go for it. His natural shot is a draw, which lends itself nicely to these circumstances. His decision is to start the ball toward the center of the green and draw it back into the pin.

Confident that he can make the shot, he visualizes it first and is then ready to make a good swing.

The middle handicap player would probably do best to play safe given this situation. Although his ball-striking skills are reasonably good, he isn't quite sure whether it's a smart idea to play for the pin—which requires a very precise shot—especially with the unforgiving water hazard lying so close. He decides that going for the pin would be too big a gamble for him and instead plans to take one more club and play for the right rear of the green. With this strategy in mind, he is reasonably sure of carrying the ball over the water, even if he doesn't get it all. If he hits his target, he'll have a long putt for a birdie and an almost sure par. If he pushes it into the trap on the right, he still has a reasonable chance of making par by making a good sand shot and is almost certain to make a five—that sure beats a six or a seven.

The high-handicap player assessing this situation would undoubtedly be apprehensive about the whole thing, since his ball-striking skills aren't on the same level as those of the more advanced players.

If he's honest with himself, he should realize that trying to play a shot close to the pin is a definite gamble. The chances are good that his shot may not go exactly where aimed and may instead find the water. Playing safe is not the best choice either, since a mishit shot from the bunker or the rough behind the green could also put him in the water.

After carefully examining the situation, he decides to play his shot well right of the green—away from both the water and the sand—to an area where he can safely pitch the ball to the green, possibly saving his par, and virtually assuring himself of a five. This is not a bad score, considering the difficulty of the hole.

That wasn't difficult, was it? Well, it always does seem that way on paper. The real test is when you're out on the course where it's very easy to let your heart make all the decisions for you.

I'm not telling you to leave your heart out of your game. I've certainly played with a lot of heart myself throughout my career. There are plenty of times on the course when you'll steer away from doing the smart thing because you know (or wish) deep down that you *can* (or *could*) make the shot, even though it's very demanding.

Take our friend the middle handicapper, who played safe on the imaginary approach. Let's take him back to that same spot again. He's well aware of what he could be in for if he tries for the pin and is off just a little. He also knows that going for the pin is a pretty big risk, even for very skilled players. But say it calls for his favorite club, a 5-iron, and that he always feels comfortable when hitting off elevated areas. Furthermore, his natural shot is a draw, which will allow him to start the ball to the right of the water and draw it back toward the pin. What I am saying is, you don't have to do the smart thing every time *if* you really feel you can make the required shot. Once again, other circumstances are a factor.

Similarly, don't ever be ashamed to play safe or even bail out if you feel the situation doesn't warrant the risk. In tournaments I've swallowed my pride and bailed out and was almost always glad I did. If you stick to your guns and put up with the few snickers that greet a super-safe shot, you'll get your share of last laughs when the scores are tallied.

DEVELOPING YOUR OWN STRATEGY

Every player should make a rule to have some kind of strategy in mind on every hole he plays before ever taking a swing. Don't just tee off without some type of goal in mind and a game plan to achieve it.

Sure, things won't always work out exactly as planned. You'll be surprised, though, at how much more confident you'll feel when addressing the ball on the tee when you have a good idea of where you want to hit it and why, instead of just swinging away.

Remember, tailor your strategy to your game. It would be nice always to play for birdie, but there are many of you who would be happy to score a bogey on most difficult holes. If that's the case, then plan a strategy to *do* just that. Plan on taking three shots to reach the green on a par four instead of forcing to make it in two. Concentrate on using the clubs you feel most comfortable with and save the others for the practice tee.

KNOW YOUR GAME AND YOUR COURSE DOWN TO THE YARD

To score your best, you've got to know how to select the right club to do the job. To do this consistently, you must know the average amount of yardage you get with every stick in your bag and not the maximum distance you can force out of each. The *average* distance is the key here.

Many amateurs base their club selection on how far they hit their clubs when they get it all. This is unrealistic when you think about it. How often do you hit a shot dead solid perfect? Be honest. Seven or eight times a round, maybe? The rest of the time you don't quite hit it solid and lose a little distance. The result is that, more often than not, the average golfer comes up short on his approach shots. This is one of the most common reasons for lost strokes.

In contrast, there isn't a professional golfer on the Tour who doesn't know exactly how far he hits each and every club in his bag. He's got to know because he can't afford to lose a stroke due to guesswork. If you want to score the best you can, then neither can you.

With the help of a friend, I recommend that you make a list of the average *carry* you get with each club, as well as the average total distance (carry plus roll). Hit at least ten shots with each club, with your friend stationed in the landing area keeping track of where each lands and where each stops. Mark the yardages in a notebook. Be sure to go through your whole bag, starting with the sand wedge and ending with the driver.

Once you've an accurate list of your yardages, use it and trust it. The next time you're out playing, choose the club that your newly acquired statistics tell you is right for the distance. I guarantee you'll be near the pin more times than you go over.

Knowing how far you hit each club isn't going to do much for your scoring if you don't also know the distance from your ball to the target. It sounds obvious, but I think that too many weekend players rely on what they feel is a pretty good idea of

AN EASY 12

I can certainly think back to times when I wished I had used my head a little more on the course instead of trying to force a tough shot. One time in particular was during the second round of the 1961 Los Angeles Open at Rancho Park Golf Course.

I had started by playing the back nine first, so when I came to the last hole, the par-five ninth, I was two under and needed only a par for a 69. But I had eagle in mind after I powdered a good drive, even though the green is tightly flanked by out of bounds fences on both sides.

Pulling out my 3-wood, I gave it a good rip, only to have the wind carry it to the right and out of bounds. I didn't give up there, however; I was still sure I could pull the shot off. This time it hooked over the left fence. Dropping another ball, I corrected for the hook and faded it over the right fence again. Down went another ball, which hooked out of bounds left. Four swings with the 3-wood, four balls out of bounds. Stubbornly I dropped my fifth ball and aimed straight at the green. It flew high and straight as a string, dropping pin high fifteen feet away. From there I two-putted for an easy 12 to finish with a 76!

the yardages on their home course instead of actually taking the time to find out. This often costs them dearly.

Every professional tournament player knows the distance to the pin from just about anywhere on the hole, because he and his caddie have put in the time during practice rounds pacing off yardages and recording them. That's a pretty good idea for every player who wants to score his best. The best way to measure yardage is to simply pace it off: The length of an average man's stride is approximately one yard long.

You'll find it well worth your time and effort to get out during a quiet time on your home course and make your own yardage book. Excluding par threes, pick two or three prominent features on every fairway—a large tree, a fairway bunker, or a sprinkler head—and measure from them to the middle of each green.

The next time you're out for a round you'll be surprised at the added confidence you'll have from eliminating the guess-work and knowing the exact yardage. It surely will help eliminate those times of uncertainty when you're not sure what club to hit, which invariably leads to a tentative swing.

If you're a typical amateur, nine times out of ten, you've too little club in your hand to get the ball up to the hole. Here's where a good knowledge of your club yardages plus your course yardages would help you cut down on being short so often. The next time you play, I'd like you to do me a favor and try something extra. *Make an effort, on every approach you make, to get the ball past the pin, whether you're shooting directly for it or not.* If that means taking one more club than you were thinking of taking or usually take, then do it. "But I'll go over the green a lot," you are probably protesting. Maybe so, but more probably *not!*

Do me this favor and *try* it. I've got a hunch you'll turn in one of the best scores you've had in quite a while.

Think. Always remember to *think* before hitting any shot. Remember the old saying about golf being 90 percent mental? Well, strategy's the area where most of that mental work needs to be done.

PART IV

SHOTMAKING AND TROUBLE SHOTS

Suppose you've reached the point where you're consistently hitting the ball fairly solidly and accurately. You've worked hard to achieve that and have been rewarded with lower scores, and with them, an even greater enjoyment of the game.

There's still improvement to be made, however. You won't be a complete player until you work some shotmaking into your game. Shotmaking is making the ball bend in either direction to different degrees when you have to; hitting it very high and soft or very low and hard when and where the situation demands.

Until you learn about shotmaking and the benefits of being able to *work* the golf ball, you won't reach your full scoring potential.

BENDING THE BALL

Rarely does a golfer hit a ball dead straight—most have one shot that is natural to them, be it a *draw*, which moves slightly from right-to-left, or a *fade*, which moves slightly from left-to-right.

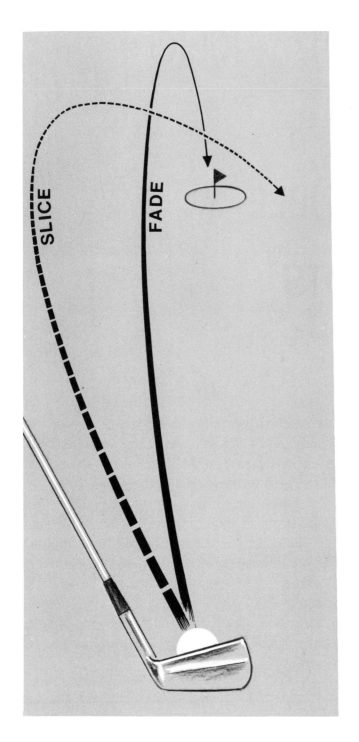

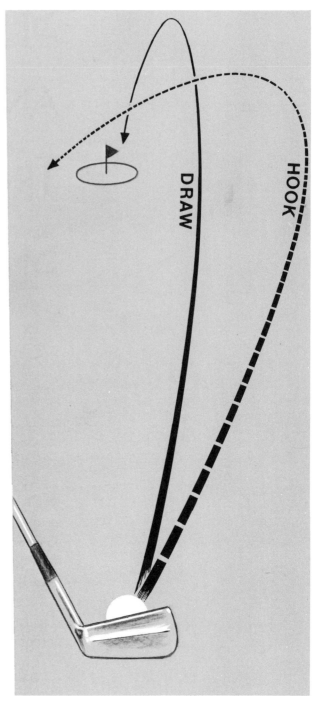

A ball that curves in the same direction as a draw but to a greater degree is called a hook; a shot that bends sharply in the same direction as a fade is called a slice. Contrary to what many amateurs believe, it's rarely an advantage to hit the ball straight to your target, for a number of reasons.

First, a lot of different factors have to come together at the precise second of impact. The club must be moving along just the right path; the clubface must be exactly square; and your timing has to be right on. Being only slightly off in any of these categories can result in a difference of as much as ten yards to either side. Your chances of being perfect every time are slight.

Using a draw or fade, though, increases your odds of getting the ball closer to the target. Say you have an approach shot of 140 yards. You decide to attempt a straight shot at the pin, hoping to put it within five yards of the hole. You have to hit the ball pretty straight to get it into your designated target area. If the shot is off by more than fifteen feet in either direction, you will have missed your target.

Now let's assume you have the same goal but decide to play a fade. This allows you to aim about about five yards left of the pin and work the ball in. If the shot moves the five yards you've visualized, you're right next to the cup, provided your distance is also correct. If it stays straight, you're still only fifteen feet away. If it fades a little more than planned, say ten yards, you're still only fifteen feet to the right of the pin.

With that game plan in mind, it's only logical to use the natural bend of the ball—be it a draw or fade—to increase your chances of hitting your target, whether it's the flag or a section of fairway.

LEARN TO WORK IT BOTH WAYS

The best thing you can do for yourself is to learn to work the ball both ways. That way, you can tailor your shot to the situation at hand.

Suppose you're facing an approach to a pin that's cut to the green's left-hand edge, which happens to be closely flanked by a bunker. If your natural shot is a fade, the way you'd normally play it would be to start the ball at the bunker and let it work back toward the pin. As you can see, you'll be in trouble if you happen to hit the ball straight.

Using a fade to increase the odds of getting closer to the target.

But if you also have the ability to hit a draw, you can attack from the opposite side, aiming to the right of the pin, and work the ball from right to left. This takes the risk of landing in the sand trap almost totally out of the shot.

Being able to hit either shot will also be helpful for control when a crosswind is blowing.

A wind blowing in the same direction as the ball is bending tends to magnify, or exaggerate, its movement, carrying a draw farther to the left than usual or a fade farther right. If you can only hit one of these shots, you'll be at the mercy of the wind if it happens to be blowing in the same direction as your shot moves.

If you're able to hit both shots, however, you'll be able to work the ball against the opposing wind, giving you a lot more control.

Each shot also emphasizes either distance or control. The spin that causes a fade is closer to actual backspin and causes the ball to fly high and land with little roll. It makes it better to play when accuracy is more important than distance. For those who are long but wild off the tee, learning to play a fade with a driver can be one of the best things you ever do for your scoring.

A ball hit with drawspin, however, will fly lower and hotter and roll more, giving you maximum distance. Many shorter hitters have added yards to their games by learning the draw.

Finally, your scoring potential will certainly increase if you can bend the ball both ways to get around trees and similar obstacles or to get into a better playing position on dogleg holes.

WHAT MAKES THE BALL CURVE?

What is it that causes a golf ball to curve in one direction or the other? The answer lies in the spin that the clubface puts on it at the moment of impact; sidespin, to be exact. Just as a baseball pitcher spins a ball sideways to throw a curve, so does a golf ball curve, either to the left or right, when the clubface puts sidespin on it.

In our discussion of backspin (on page 50), you'll remember that, basically, the more loft on a club, the more backspin it produces. Now, the more backspin you put on a ball, the more it negates the effect of sidespin. Conversely, the less backspin you put on a ball, the more the effect of sidespin.

This is why, if you're hooking or slicing your driver, going to a 4-wood off the tee can straighten you out to a certain degree. It also explains why it's easy to slice a driver or long iron but not a wedge.

It's the *angle* of the clubface at impact in relation to the swing path that imparts sidespin to the ball. If the face is open, you get slice spin; if the face is closed, hookspin.

The *amount of spin* put on the ball determines how severely it will curve—the more spin, the sharper the bend in the shot. The degree of spin is determined mainly by how much the clubface is open or closed at the moment of impact. The more open the face, the more slice-spin produced, while the more closed the face, the more hookspin produced.

Knowing what causes a ball to fade, slice, draw, and hook is helpful to understanding the minor swing adjustments it takes to hit these shots.

You won't be a complete golfer until you learn how.

12
The Shots

PLAYING A DRAW

To hit a draw, start by getting into the right address position by aligning your body to the right of your target in a *closed* position.

Close your stance by pulling your right foot, hip, and shoulder back a couple of inches from being square to the target line. You may find it easier to simply pick out an object slightly right of your actual target and set your body up as if you were aiming directly for it. Align the leading edge of the clubface, however, squarely at your original target before taking your grip. Doing this sets the clubface slightly closed in relation to the line set by your body that you'll be swinging on. On impact this will give you the necessary counterclockwise spin on the ball to make it curve slightly from right to left.

You don't have to make any other adjustments—just swing as you normally do and you'll put the necessary degree of spin on the ball and produce a draw.

PLAYING A HOOK

A sharp hook is an unfavorable golf shot when hit unintentionally. Knowing what causes it and how to play it, however, gives any player a powerful weapon for getting out of trouble situations and safely onto or near the green.

Hitting a hook demands putting the same type of sidespin on the ball as on a draw but to a much greater degree. Close your stance even more than you would for a draw and close the clubface slightly in relation to your original target line before taking your grip.

To play an intentional hook, start by addressing the ball in a very closed stance.

Take the club away on a more inside path than usual.

Bringing the club back inside will result in
a flatter swing plane than normal.

Swing the club down and through on an
inside-out path, swinging the clubhead
through to the right of the target and
following through "low and around."

You should finish with the hands lower
than normal.

On the takeaway, bring your club back on a more inside path rather than straight back away from the ball.

On the downswing, make an effort to swing on an inside-out path. Concentrate on swinging your club through the ball and out to the right of the target. As a result, your follow-through will be lower than normal. Your hands not finishing above your left shoulder but rather pointing straight away from your chest.

The shot will start well right, but will curve sharply to the left and land with a lot of roll.

PLAYING A FADE

To hit a fade, set up in an open address position, as you would for the short irons, by pulling the left foot back from square by about two inches; do the same with the hips and shoulders.

Align the clubface squarely to the original target line, making it slightly open in relation to the line you're aiming your body. Then take your grip.

From here, swing normally. You'll impart the needed fade-spin, producing a gentle, controllable fade.

PLAYING A SLICE

Like the hook, the slice, or banana ball as it's sometimes called, is usually a shot to be dreaded, but knowing how to hit one when the situation calls for it can prove extremely valuable.

To hit a slice, again, you'll want to put the same type of sidespin on the ball as you did with the fade, but to a greater degree. Doing this requires that you open your stance a little more than you did for the fade and then open the clubface slightly in relation to the original target line.

On the takeaway, concentrate on pushing your club back on an outside line instead of straight away and on bringing your club down on an outside-in downswing path, cutting across the ball through impact. To help you do this, think of swinging the club down through the ball and following through to the left of the target.

The ball will start to the left, then slice sharply back toward the right, landing without much roll.

Playing a slice reduces the distance you normally get with whatever club you use, so be sure you take a much stronger club than normal, a 5-iron, for example, instead of a 7-iron.

To play an intentional slice, start by addressing the ball in a very open stance.

Take the club away on a more outside path than usual.

Bringing the club back on an outside path automatically results in a more upright swing plane.

Make the downswing on an outside-in path, swinging the clubhead through to the left of the target.

The hands will be lower than normal in the finish.

LOW SHOT

Knowing how to hit a low shot, or punch as it's often called, is extremely valuable in several typical playing situations.

One is where you have an obstacle close in front of you, say, one or more overhanging tree branches. You aren't far enough away from them to either go over the tree or bend the ball around it. Your best escape is to go underneath them.

Another situation is the approach shot in either a stiff crosswind or a headwind. Instead of getting the ball up high and letting the wind toss it around, play a low, hard shot that bores into and under the wind. This gives you more control and increases your chances of putting the ball exactly where you want it.

The low shot also is effective on a very firm and dry course. It's better to hit short of the green and run the ball to the pin. This is, of course, provided there are no hazards to prevent you from doing so.

To hit a low punch, take a club two or three clubs stronger than you normally would from that particular distance.

Choke up for control. Open your stance and play the ball back around center or even a little behind center if you prefer. Set your hands well ahead of the ball and swing straight back and through, punching down into it with a limited follow-through.

Concentrate on keeping your head very still and your body fairly quiet throughout the entire motion. It's mainly an arms-and-hands action.

The ball will fly low and hard and land with lots of run.

The low shot: My goal in this situation is to hit a low, hard shot that flies underneath the branches, lands short and rolls up to the green.

Choke down and set up open, playing the ball back and setting the hands well ahead of it.

Swing the club straight back, keeping the head and body still.

Make a hard downswing with the arms and hands.

"Punch through" the ball into a limited follow-through.

HIGH SHOT

The average golfer doesn't realize just how quickly and sharply it's possible to make a golf ball rise. All it takes is the proper technique, and knowing it can help save a stroke once in a while when a tree is blocking your way to the green.

To hit a high shot, set up with a very open stance, the ball positioned well forward, your hands set ahead of it, and the clubface open. For an even higher shot, set your hands back a little farther to increase the effective loft of the club.

The high shot: In this situation, I want the ball to rise sharply, carry over the tree and drop onto the green.

Set up in a very open stance, with the ball positioned well forward and the clubface open.

Make a normal backswing.

The key to getting the ball up quickly is to concentrate on moving your right shoulder down and through the shot on the downswing, while thinking of trying to slide the clubface underneath the ball at impact. It's important not to let your right hand roll over your left. Pull through strongly with your left hand to keep the clubface open as it slides under and through.

The resulting shot will rise sharply, fly high, and land with very little roll.

Concentrate on keeping the right shoulder moving down and through the ball on the downswing.

Slide the clubface under the ball, pulling through hard with the left hand to keep the right hand from rolling over the left until well into the follow-through.

Coast to a smooth, high finish.

13
Hilly Lies

B ack in chapter ten I mentioned that putting would certainly be a lot easier if every green were flat. Well, I guess the same logic applies to the fairways, too. It would sure make the game a lot easier if we could hit every shot off level ground.

The game wasn't meant to be that easy though, and the fact is, many of the courses in the United States *are* relatively flat compared to the rolling fairways of the links courses in Scotland, where the game was invented.

One way to handle hilly lies better is simply to avoid them. Most holes, even those with a lot of contours to their fairways, have level areas you can always target your drives toward. Carefully surveying each hole for that level target area and then being able to hit the ball there will save you the trouble of playing from an uneven lie.

Still, no one can avoid hilly lies forever. Knowing how to play them is crucial to becoming a complete golfer.

There are four types of hilly lies: ball above the feet; ball below the feet; uphill lie; and downhill lie. Hitting successful shots from each lie mainly is a matter of understanding how the different slopes affect the address position and swing and of making the proper adjustments for each. You also have to understand how the adjustments you make to hit each of them will affect the final outcome of your shot.

BALL ABOVE FEET

Playing a ball that lies above your feet requires that you not only stand farther away from it but stand straighter than normal at address. How much farther depends upon how much higher the ball is above the level of the ground on which you're standing.

Standing farther from the ball automatically forces you to make a flatter swing, causing a right-to-left trajectory. So be sure to aim to the right of the target and plan for the ball to work itself back to the left. How much the ball moves depends upon how flat you swing, which in turn is due to how much higher the ball lies in relation to your feet.

To help you keep your balance, place your weight on the balls of your feet and choke down on the club for control.

When playing this shot or any one that requires you to assume a much different address position than normal, always take a couple of practice swings so that you get a feel for the motion that's required.

Remember to play it smart under extreme circumstances. If the slope is so severe that your address is very awkward, swing easily.

BALL BELOW FEET

A ball lying below your feet forces you to stand closer to it and bend your waist more than usual. Just how much closer to the ball you have to stand is determined by how much lower it is in relation to where your feet are. The lower the ball, the closer you have to position yourself and the more you have to bend to get the clubhead down to it.

Since you have to bend farther forward than normal to play this shot, it's a good idea to set your weight back on your heels and to keep your chin up to prevent yourself from toppling forward. Also, hold your club at the end of the grip.

Because this kind of lie forces you closer to the ball at address, your swing plane will be more upright, leading to a right-to-left trajectory on the shot. The lower the ball and the closer you stand, the more the shot will fade.

A ball above the feet forces you to stand slightly farther from it than usual. Place your weight a little forward on the balls of your feet for balance and choke down for control.

Standing farther from the ball forces a flatter swing plane, causing a shot that moves from right-to-left.

Keep your head from dipping even slightly
to avoid hitting "fat."

Emphasize swinging into a good, balanced position in the finish.

A ball below the feet requires that you stand closer to the ball than usual. Keep your weight back toward the heels for balance and hold the club at the very end of the grip.

Standing closer to the ball causes a very upright swing plane, producing a shot that moves from left to right.

How much the ball bends depends on
how steeply the slope dictates you swing.

Strive to keep your balance all the way to
the finish.

UPHILL LIE

When hitting off an uphill slope you'll want to compensate for the slope's angle by flexing your left knee more than usual in order to set the line of your hips and shoulders as close to normal, or level, as you can. The steeper the slope, the more you must flex your knee. Play the ball a little farther forward in the stance than usual.

When hitting off an uphill lie, compensate for the slope by flexing the left knee a little more than usual.

The weight will tend to stay back on the right foot throughout the swing, so take a shorter backswing than usual.

Your weight tends to hang back on your right foot through impact due to the slope. This results in a right-to-left ball flight. You can counteract this tendency to some extent by taking a shorter backswing than usual and emphasizing the follow-through. As a general rule, the steeper the slope, the more your weight stays back and the more the ball will curve. So, allow for it.

Because the weight stays back on the right side, the hands will release sooner, causing the ball to curve from right to left.

Make up for the shorter backswing by emphasizing a strong follow-through.

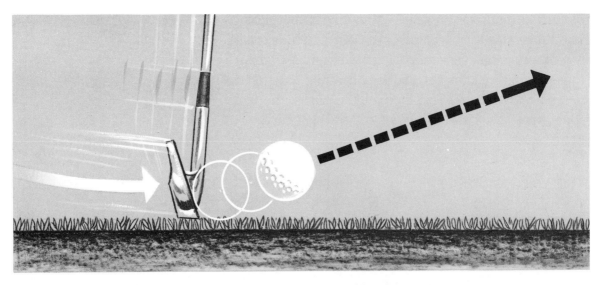

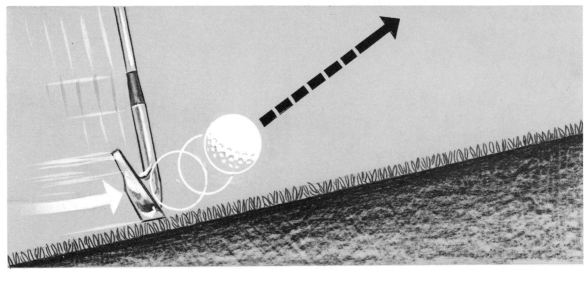

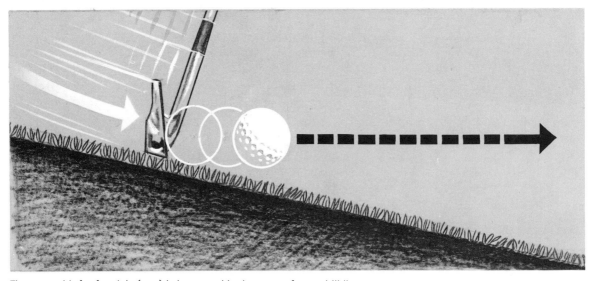

The normal loft of a club (top) is increased in the case of an uphill lie
(middle) and decreased in the case of a downhill lie (bottom).

Hitting the ball in the direction of the upward angle of the slope also alters the height and distance of the shot by making it fly higher and shorter than it normally does from level ground. Allow for this by taking more club. The steeper the hill, the more extra club you'll need.

DOWNHILL LIE

Compensate for a downhill lie by flexing your right knee. The goal is to set the line of your hips and shoulders as close to level as possible.

Make your best effort to swing normally, paying special attention to your backswing and downswing to keep from catching the ground with the clubhead. To increase your chances of hitting the ball instead of the ground first, position the ball back a little farther than usual in your stance. Be sure you keep your chin up—drop your head and you'll hit fat.

The angle of the downslope encourages a quick weight shift to your left foot during the downswing, resulting in a left-to-right ball flight. The steeper the slope, the more the ball will curve.

The angle of the downslope also affects the height and direction of the shot. It tends to deloft the club, that is, giving a 5-iron the effective loft of a 4- or even a 3-iron. The more severe the slope of the hill, the more it delofts the club. Because of this, whatever club you choose will fly lower and longer than it normally would from a level lie.

Only use low-lofted fairway woods, such as the 3- and 4-wood and long irons, from slightly downhill lies. More severe lies demand a wood or iron with enough loft to get the ball airborne.

When hitting off a downhill lie, compensate for the slope by flexing the right knee
more than usual.

Take special care not to catch the ground
with the clubhead on both the backswing
or the downswing.

Make an extra effort to stay down and extend the club low through impact.

The angle of the slope promotes a quick weight shift to the left on the downswing, delaying the release of the hands and causing the ball to move from left-to-right.

14
Trouble Shots

The last thing any golfer wants to see on a Sunday morning outing is a ball buried in a bunker, lying low in deep rough or under water. Sooner or later, no matter how good a player you are, you'll get into trouble. Everyone does.

The difference between good trouble players and not-so-good ones is that the good ones have taken the time to learn the necessary techniques while the not-so-good ones haven't even considered them. The good ones accept trouble as part of the game and know that grousing about it won't help.

Every player would benefit from adopting the positive attitude of the good player. Don't whine about your bad luck. Instead, think of the trouble as a challenge and focus on playing a good recovery shot.

The game could get pretty boring if you never got into trouble. I'm sure a lot of you probably are thinking you could use that kind of boredom! Whenever I've managed to pull off a good trouble shot, I've found it very satisfying. With the right attitude, it can almost become a pleasure.

In this chapter, I've chosen some of the most common trouble situations along with a couple of not-so-common ones that are good to know about. Take note of the techniques and put some practice time in. You'll find trouble a lot easier to tackle in the future.

SAND PLAY

Explosion Shot from Greenside Sand

Time and time again golfers hear that the explosion shot from sand is the easiest shot in golf. This statement alone must increase their apprehension when they step into a bunker. Fearfully, they think, "If this is supposed to be such an easy shot, I sure don't want to screw it up like I did the last one . . ."

They usually allow their fear to get the better of them and spoil their concentration. Rushing to get the worst over with, they end up making their worst effort.

Most amateurs play poorly from sand because they neither understand how to play the shot nor have had enough experience with it. Probably the last time the average weekend player practiced a sand shot was the last time he was in a bunker. There's no getting around it, you have to practice sand shots to be a good sand player.

To play a normal explosion shot from a greenside bunker, take a sand wedge and assume a very narrow, open stance—so open that your body is almost facing the target. Dig your feet in to establish a firm base. Digging in will result in the ball being slightly above your feet, so choke down on the club to compensate for this. Play the ball off your left heel and open the blade of the sand wedge. Remember not to ground the club or, in other words, touch the sand with it except when hitting the shot. Grounding a club in a hazard is a one-shot penalty. Concentrate on making a smooth swing and aim to hit the sand *behind* the ball. Be sure to follow through. Keep the clubface open through impact; don't allow your right hand to roll over your left. This is mainly a hands-and-arms shot, so keep your lower body still. Work on keeping your head very still.

Control how soft or hard the trajectory of the shot is by varying the amount you open the face of the club. Open it more for a higher, softer landing shot, less for one that flies lower and harder.

The fact is that the club never actually strikes the ball on an explosion shot but only the area of sand it rests on. Your ball won't spring off the clubface the way it does on a normal shot. Instead, it will come out more softly in relation to the force of the swing used. This means you must hit only the sand with a slightly harder swing than you'd use to pitch the ball from the

To play a normal explosion shot, take a narrow, extremely open stance, play the ball off your left heel and open the blade of your sand wedge.

Make a smooth backswing, picking the club up quickly with the arms and hands while keeping the body still.

Hit down just behind the ball, keeping the
blade open through impact and making
sure to follow through.

GARY PLAYER'S FINEST SAND SHOT

I don't suppose that Gary Player will ever forget the sand shot he played at the seventy-second hole in the 1961 Masters at Augusta National Golf Club in Augusta, Georgia. "The man in black" had led me by four shots going into the last round and had posted a smooth thirty-four on the front side. On the back, he ran into trouble. A bogey at ten was followed by a double-bogey at thirteen and another bogey at fifteen. At eighteen, Gary put his second shot in the right-hand bunker but managed to blast the ball to six feet and hole the putt for a two-over par 74 and a total of 280. At that point, he told me later, he felt he had thrown the tournament away.

Gary's problems had given me a one-shot lead, which I held going into the last hole. After a great drive at eighteen, my friends in the gallery came up to slap me on the back. I couldn't miss. All I needed was a par four for victory, a five for a tie. With these thoughts in mind I hit my 7-iron to the green. I came off the shot and pushed it into the same bunker Gary had been in earlier. Then I blasted over the green, putted it from there fifteen feet past the cup and then missed the putt that would have tied Player; scoring a double-bogey six.

I had made the fatal error of enjoying the victory before I'd earned it and lost my concentration. Looking back and considering the disasters he'd encountered on the back nine, that was some bunker shot Gary played.

same distance, trusting that the ball will be removed along with its cushion of sand.

Don't try to overpower this shot. Allow the club to do the work. Keep your downswing smooth, while making sure to accelerate. The rhythm should be similar to pitching a ball underhanded. Any deceleration on this shot destroys your chances of safely getting the ball out.

Sand Textures

The texture of the sand determines club selection. You can feel this texture with your feet when you dig in to play the shot.

Most sand is fairly soft and fluffy, making the sand wedge the club of choice from a normal lie. Its large flange (the bottom of the clubhead) prevents it from digging too deeply into the sand. Instead, it rides through just below the surface, exploding the cushion of sand the ball is on—and the ball with it—out of the trap.

If the sand texture is firm, because it's naturally coarse and hard or wet, it's a good idea not to use the sand wedge, since the flange might bounce off the harder surface and belly the ball—when the edge of the clubface strikes the ball near its equator, causing the shot to fly very hard and low.

In a case like this, go with a pitching wedge. Its smaller flange and sharper edged face are designed to dig into hard sand rather than bounce off it. Use the same technique as with the sand wedge.

Long Explosion Shot

For a long explosion shot from say, thirty-five to forty yards away, you address the ball with a narrow, slightly less open stance than for a short explosion. Play the ball in the middle of your stance or slightly farther back, hands slightly ahead. Be sure to dig your feet in firmly to maintain balance on the harder swing you have to take.

The key difference between the long and the short explosion is in opening the face of the sand wedge slightly, depending upon the distance you want to hit it. It's important also to make a shallower, more sweeping swing going back and coming through to keep from digging too deeply into the sand and to drive the ball in a more forward direction.

Use a wider, less open stance for a long explosion shot, playing the ball toward the middle or slightly back and opening the blade just a little.

Make a shallower, more sweeping back-swing and downswing to take less sand and drive the ball forward on a lower trajectory.

Accelerate through the shot, making sure you follow through to guarantee getting the ball up and out.

As on all shots, keep the head down and still, raising it only after the ball has left the clubface.

Buried Bunker Shot

A fried egg lie or worse, one that's almost totally buried, is no picnic. The main objective on this shot is to get the ball out onto the green somewhere. If the ball finishes close, that's a bonus, since this is one of the toughest shots that any golfer will face.

Use the pitching wedge to play a buried ball. Take a slightly open stance, close the face of the club and make an upright swing, picking the club up quickly with your hands and

To dig the ball out of a buried lie, use a pitching wedge, instead of a sand wedge, for its sharper edged face. Take a narrow, slightly open stance, play the ball off the left heel and close the blade.

wrists and coming down hard about an inch behind the ball. The idea is to cut sharply into the sand then under the ball, jarring it up and out.

Concentrate on making a follow-through, although there probably won't be much of one because of the depth you have to dig. Thinking about making a follow-through forces you to accelerate down into the sand, which is essential for success.

Pick the club up sharply on the backswing with the hands and wrists.

Hit down hard about an inch behind the ball. Closing the face allows the leading edge of the club to cut into the sand and slide underneath the ball.

Fairway Sand Shot

Fairway trap shots aren't as hard as they appear.

Ideally, you should get the ball from the trap to the green or advance the ball as far forward as possible. Before commit-

From a fairway sand trap, set up open, digging the feet in to establish a firm base. Play the ball slightly farther back than usual with the hands well ahead and the blade square.

You may want to make only a three-quarter swing for control.

ting yourself, carefully examine both the lie and the position of the forward lip of the trap to determine your chances of meeting your goal. You may have to settle for less.

Swing down on a low, sweeping path, making sure to hit the ball before the sand.

Follow through, and the ball will be removed cleanly from the sand.

The ball may be in a fried egg lie or, worse, buried. Common sense tells you that your chances of moving it far aren't very good. In this case, take your sand wedge and make sure you get the ball out of the bunker and into a good position on the fairway.

Even if the lie is good, always be sure to gauge the height of the forward lip of the trap. The club you select must have enough loft to clear it, even if that means laying up short of your intended target.

To play a fairway bunker shot from a normal lie, take special care to dig in and get a firm base with your feet first, since balance throughout the swing is crucial to the shot. Assume a slightly open stance and play the ball back a little more, with your hands ahead and the blade square.

Unlike the explosion shots, this shot requires you to hit the ball before the sand. Any sand that gets between the blade and the ball will ruin your shot. With that caveat in mind, make a special effort to keep your head very still while making a very shallow takeaway and downswing path to sweep the ball cleanly from the sand.

Because clubhead control is so important on this shot and the margin for error is so small, you may want to make only a three-quarter swing.

I'm often asked if it's all right to use a wood from a fairway trap. My answer is yes, provided the ball is lying cleanly and the lip is low enough to clear. Then go ahead, remembering, as with all fairway trap shots, to set up with an open stance and to strike the ball first.

OUT OF THE ROUGH

The most common trouble shot you'll face is getting out of the high grass, or rough, that borders fairways and some greens. On most courses, the rough is cut at various heights. Generally, the farther off the fairway you go, the deeper the rough gets. That means you have to know how to handle different degrees of rough.

Light Rough

When situated in light rough, you usually won't have too much problem getting your clubhead through the grass. Any grass between the ball and the clubface, however, will greatly reduce the amount of spin on the ball compared to the spin you'd get from a normal lie. So plan on the ball releasing quickly and rolling more than it would from a good lie.

On longer shots from light rough, avoid using the long irons in favor of using the well-lofted fairway woods, like the 4- or 5-wood. Their larger heads tend to spread the grass and slide through it, whereas the long irons usually snare in the grass, making it difficult to get through the ball.

A CRUCIAL SHOT FROM WET ROUGH

With a few holes left to play, I was leading the British Open at Royal Birkdale in England in 1961 and was trying to stave off the tenacious challenge of the fine Welsh golfer Dai Rees. Then, my tee shot on the par-four fifteenth was blown astray by the heavy winds that had been present all week and deposited into the right-hand rough.

I found the ball lying deep in the tangled high grass, which was also wet from a light rain. My one option, it appeared, was to accept the limitations of the lie and wedge back to the fairway. I knew that that would increase my chances of making bogey, which would give Rees a chance to gain on me.

I took my 6-iron and went for the green rather than play safe. I tore into the shot as hard as I could, knowing I had to hit the ball with everything I had to get it out and avoid leaving it or putting it in a worse position. The blade slashed through the grass and blasted the ball toward the green, leaving a divot mark a foot long. Two putts later I had par, which eventually helped me edge Rees out by one stroke for the title.

Heavy Rough

When the ball is lying in heavy, or deep, rough, you have to resign yourself to the fact that there's really only so much you'll be able to do with it.

The best asset you can have to get the ball out of heavy rough is a strong pair of hands to power the club down and through the thick grass.

To play the shot, choose an iron and close the blade to make it sharper for cutting through the grass. Take a very firm grip, and otherwise the setup is normal.

Out of heavy rough, set up normally—
slightly open, ball off the left heel, hands
ahead but with the blade a little closed.

Take your club back straight, maintaining the closed position on the backswing. Come down as hard as you can, keeping the head still, of course. As the clubface goes through the ball, the grass will force it back to a square position. Make a strong follow-through to free the ball.

Extremely deep rough may call for the pitching wedge or 9-iron, since the combination of a descending swing along with a sharp-edged clubface is the only way to get the ball out safely. If so, accept your fate and concentrate on getting back onto the fairway.

On the backswing, take the club straight back, keeping the clubface closed.

Come down as hard as you can on the downswing while keeping a steady head.

For solid contact, make an extra effort to stay down through impact.

It's crucial that you follow through on the shot to move the ball out of the thick grass.

OFF HARDPAN

You'll run into hardpan—a bald spot of ground baked hard by the sun—more often in warmer climates than you will in cooler ones.

Playing a shot from hardpan is similar to the way you'd hit a ball from a fairway bunker—you must hit the ball first using a very sweeping type of swing.

To increase your chances of doing this, set up as you normally would but play the ball farther back in your stance, with your hands well ahead. Keep your head very still and make a deliberate backswing.

The resulting shot will fly lower and harder than normal, so be sure to allow for this.

Off hardpan, set up normally, but with the ball a little farther back than usual and the hands well ahead.

Make a slow, shallow backswing, keeping the head very still.

Sweep the ball off the surface as you would from fairway sand, making sure to hit the ball first.

Allow for the shot to fly lower and harder than usual.

FROM A DIVOT HOLE

It's unfortunate, but every so often you hit a good drive only to have it come to rest in a divot hole on the fairway: an indentation in the turf where someone previously took a divot and didn't replace it. This is a tough break that's hard to take in stride, but do your best.

To play the shot, set up to the ball normally, but with a square or slightly closed blade. The object is to hit down on the ball very hard, hitting the ball first and then digging into the turf. Don't be afraid of tearing up the ground a little—the greenkeeper won't mind.

To help make the hard but controlled downswing necessary for this shot, concentrate on making a very slow, deliberate backswing; focusing on setting your hands at the top before coming down.

The resulting shot will fly lower and with more roll than from a normal lie.

To play the ball out of a divot hole, set up normally, but with a square or slightly closed blade (on more severe lies).

Make a slow, deliberate backswing, focusing on setting the hands in position at the top before coming down.

Hit down on the ball hard, hitting the ball first with a forceful but controlled downswing.

Squaring the blade helps it dig down into the turf to get the ball out of the hole.

The shot will fly lower than usual and land
with more roll.

THE "FLYING" LIE

Every once in a while you get a fairway lie where a few taller blades of grass or clover come between your ball and the clubface. Anything getting in the way of absolutely clean club-to-ball contact reduces the amount of backspin on the shot. When this happens, the ball doesn't rise as high as it normally

To play a shot from a "flying" lie, take one club less than usual and set up normally, closing the blade slightly.

Make a normal swing.

does, but instead flies, going lower and farther with more than usual run.

From this type of lie, take one less club and close the blade slightly to allow the leading edge to cut through the grass behind the ball.

Slightly closing the clubface helps the leading edge cut through whatever stands between it and the ball.

Because less backspin is imparted on the ball at impact, it will tend to fly lower and farther and land with more run than usual.

THE PERCHED LIE

You occasionally may find your ball perched on high grass, or rough, instead of sitting down in it.

Play this shot by choking down on the club and standing a little taller to the ball than usual. This brings up the clubhead to the same level as the ball.

To play the ball from a perched lie, choke down on the club and stand slightly taller than usual, taking special care not to disturb anything with the clubhead that could cause the ball to fall.

Make a low takeaway and deliberate backswing, guarding against any upward or downward movement of the head.

Take special care not to disturb anything around the ball when addressing it. It could easily fall from its precarious position and will cost you a penalty stroke if it does.

Make a very deliberate backswing and keep your head very still, guarding especially against any downward movement that might result in the clubhead passing underneath the ball. Make a low takeaway and shallow downswing to sweep the ball squarely from its perch.

The downswing should be on a shallow path to sweep the ball squarely from its perch.

Swing into a high follow-through.

PLAYING THE LEFT-HANDED SHOT

This is another tricky situation in which you may find yourself every once in a while. The ball comes to rest next to a tree or similar object, preventing you from taking your normal right-handed stance.

Instead of taking an unplayable lie, you might try playing the shot left-handed.

To do so, take one of the broader-faced clubs, such as the sand or pitching wedge, turn it upside down and address the ball from the opposite side.

Don't worry about getting the grip perfect, but be sure to reverse your hand position, putting your left hand lower on the club than your right. Take several practice swings to get the feel of the swing, concentrating on pushing back and pulling through with your right hand.

Set up to the ball however you feel most comfortable, but be sure the clubface is squarely behind the ball at address. The main objective here is to put the clubface on the ball and get it out of there and not to whiff it. So keep your head *very* still.

You should make fairly decent contact, which is pretty much all you should be hoping for when playing this kind of shot. It is, I'd like to add, a good one to practice before trying out on the course.

WATER SHOTS

The Water Explosion

Every player sometime or another hits a shot into a water hazard, only to find it near the surface, appearing playable. What do you do? Try to save yourself the penalty stroke but risk a high score if the shot doesn't come off?

My advice is to assess the situation very carefully. As a rule, if more than one-half of the ball is submerged, discretion is usually the better part of valor. Take the penalty.

If less than half of the ball is lying below the surface and if you're able to take a decent stance (even if it means taking one or both shoes off), then you may want to give it a try. Once you've made the decision to play the ball, be confident about it. There are few things worse than trying to save a stroke but

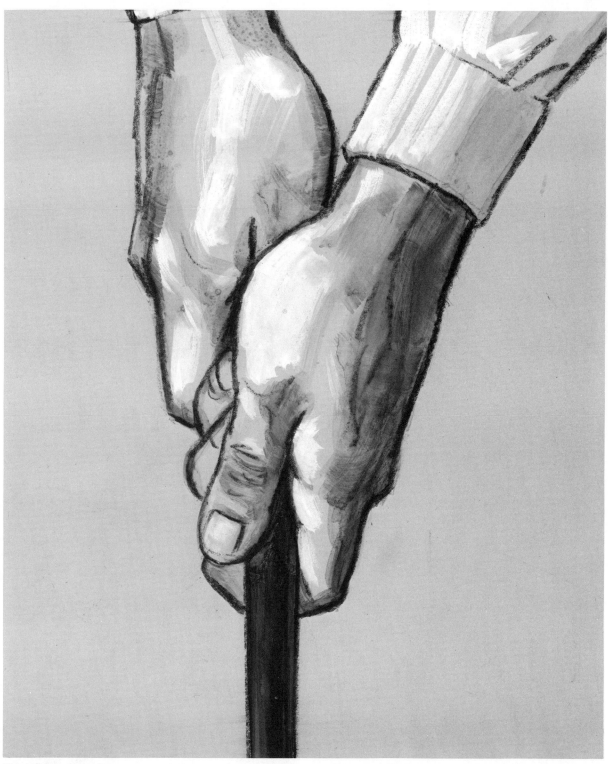

The left-handed grip.

To play a left-handed shot, take a broad-faced club like a sand wedge, turn it upside down and address the ball from the opposite side, making sure the club-face is squarely behind the ball at address.

Concentrate on keeping the head very still and pushing the club back with the right hand on the backswing.

Pull the club through the ball on the downswing, making a big effort to contact the ball solidly.

end up wasting more instead because you took a tentative, decelerating swing.

If you do decide to go for it, be prepared to go all out and spray some water. Because of this, be smart and don your rain gear first. It's a tough enough shot to play without getting soaked over it!

Take your sand wedge and set your hands well forward. Be sure to close the blade so it doesn't skid off the surface but rather cuts down into it. Pick the club up sharply on a very upright plane and knife the blade into the water about an inch behind the ball on a sharp downswing angle.

The water will slow the blade up quickly, so swing hard and follow through. Like the explosion shot from sand, your goal is to remove the cushion of water the ball is lying in so that the ball comes out with it.

Walking on Water

This shot will come up rarely in the lives of most weekend golfers, but in case it does in yours, here's how to make the ball skip across a pond like a stone, or make it walk on water.

The idea is to hit the ball very hard and low, trying to make it fly as close to horizontal, or parallel to the water, as possible so it will just kiss off the water several times before jumping out on the other side. It has to be hit very hard because each skip will take a lot off the ball.

It helps to be close to the water's edge to play the shot. Take a low-lofted club, such as a 3- or 4-iron and play the ball back in your stance. Set your hands ahead of the ball and slightly open the blade. Make a compact backswing and punch hard into the back of the ball, keeping your wrists very firm to prevent the club from releasing through impact.

You *must* prevent your hands from turning over through the ball, because any kind of hookspin on the ball will cause it to dive down into the depths.

This is obviously a low percentage shot. I would only risk it if, say, I were in a match and had nothing to lose but that particular hole. You may find yourself in the same situation someday, where, say, some tree branches in front of you prevent lofting the ball high to a green lying just on the other side of a pond. To punch the ball over the water will definitely put you over the green—so why not try to skip the ball?

Good luck if you do!

To play a shot out of water, pick the club up sharply on a very upright plane and knife the blade into the water about an inch behind the ball, make a strong followthrough.

Conclusion

NOW IT'S UP TO YOU

I've done my part. I've taught you the Five Fundamentals of the golf swing. They are the same ones that my father taught me. To quickly review them: the one right grip, the proper address position, the one-piece takeaway, the importance of keeping your head still throughout the swing, and accelerating through the ball.

I've told you how to play each individual club, how to play the shots around the green and save strokes in the scoring zone, how to develop a good putting stroke and strategy, and how to improve your green reading.

We've covered the mental side of the game and how to come up with a playing strategy that's right for you. We've explored the areas of better decision making that will ultimately lead to lower scores, and how using your mind to visualize your shots enables you to play each and every hole better. Then there was shotmaking—working the ball varying degrees from right to left and left to right, handling hilly lies and trouble shots in general. We went through all that.

So now you're through reading and are ready to play great golf, right?

Or are you?

I guess I did forget to mention the section on practice. That's what's left now that your reading is over. It's the bridge between what you've learned in this book and making it a reality.

You can achieve my promise of knocking ten to fifteen strokes off your game, but *only* by taking what you've learned with your mind here and teaching it to your body.

So get started. I promise that you'll be glad you did.